Selected Poems

Selected Poems

CONRAD AIKEN

SCHOCKEN BOOKS · NEW YORK

First published by Schocken Books 1982
10 9 8 7 6 5 4 3 2 1   82 83 84 85
Published by agreement with Oxford University Press
Copyright © 1918, 1920, 1925, 1930, 1931, 1932, 1933, 1934,
1935, 1936, 1942, 1945, 1947, 1949, 1953, 1955, 1958, 1959, 1960,
1961 by Conrad Aiken

"Landscape West of Eden," Copyright 1942 by *American Poetry Journal*.

Permission to include "Mayflower," "Hallowe'en," and "The Crystal"
has been granted by Thomas Yoseloff, The Sagamore Press. The
Hogarth Press has granted permission (for the British Isles) to include
"Senlin: A Biography."

Library of Congress Cataloging in Publication Data
Aiken, Conrad, 1889-1973.
    Selected poems.
    Reprint. Originally published: New York: Oxford
University Press, 1961.
    Includes index.
    I. Title.
[PS3501.I5A6 1982]   811'.52   82-3234   AACR2

Manufactured in the United States of America
ISBN 0-8052-0718-X

Preface

The arrangement of the poems in this book is for the most part chronological, the one major exception being that of *The Coming Forth by Day of Osiris Jones*. This was actually written after *Preludes for Memnon*, and before *Time in the Rock*; but I have now placed it ahead of those poems, and for two reasons. For one thing, it helps, I think, to explain those two sequences; and for another, it enables me to put them together, as they were meant to be—to all intents, they are one poem.

For the rest I think I need only say that limitations of space have inevitably caused the omission of a good many things that I would have liked to include. Less than half of the *Preludes* are here, but they keep their proper serial numbers, and therefore the reader who cares to do so can refer to the *Collected Poems* to see them in context. Of the six early "symphonies" which comprise the long poem, *The Divine Pilgrim*, published by the University of Georgia Press, only two are here given in their entirety, *Senlin: A Biography*, and *Changing Mind*. Too long to include, and virtually impossible to represent by selection or fragmentation, the others are best left to themselves. The sole exceptions are the two first poems in the book, which are taken from *The House of Dust*, written in 1917, and are the earliest work here presented. *The Crystal*, at the end of the book, 1958, is the latest.

The explanatory notes for *Senlin: A Biography* and *The Kid*, not here included, may be found at the end of *Collected Poems*.

C. A.

Brewster, Massachusetts, 1960

Contents

Selected Poems

Palimpsest: The Deceitful Portrait

Well, as you say, we live for small horizons:
We move in crowds, we flow and talk together,
Seeing so many eyes and hands and faces,
So many mouths, and all with secret meanings,—
Yet know so little of them; only seeing
The small bright circle of our consciousness,
Beyond which lies the dark. Some few we know—
Or think we know. Once, on a sun-bright morning,
I walked in a certain hallway, trying to find
A certain door: I found one, tried it, opened,
And there in a spacious chamber, brightly lighted,
A hundred men played music, loudly, swiftly,
While one tall woman sent her voice above them
In powerful incantation . . . Closing then the door
I heard it die behind me, fade to whisper,—
And walked in a quiet hallway as before.
Just such a glimpse, as through that opened door,
Is all we know of those we call our friends.
We hear a sudden music, see a playing
Of ordered thoughts—and all again is silence.
The music, we suppose (as in ourselves)
Goes on forever there, behind shut doors,—
As it continues after our departure,
So, we divine, it played before we came.
What do you know of me, or I of you?
Little enough . . . We set these doors ajar
Only for chosen movements of the music:
This passage (so I think—yet this is guesswork)
Will please him,—it is in a strain he fancies,—
More brilliant, though, than his; and while he likes it
He will be piqued . . . He looks at me bewildered

And thinks (to judge from self—this too is guesswork)
The music strangely subtle, deep in meaning,
Perplexed with implications; he suspects me
Of hidden riches, unexpected wisdom.
Or else I let him hear a lyric passage,—
Simple and clear; and all the while he listens
I make pretence to think my doors are closed.
This too bewilders him. He eyes me sidelong
Wondering 'Is he such a fool as this?
Or only mocking?'—There I let it end.
Sometimes, of course, and when we least suspect it—
When we pursue our thoughts with too much passion,
Talking with too great zeal—our doors fly open
Without intention; and the hungry watcher
Stares at the feast, carries away our secrets,
And laughs . . . but this, for many counts, is seldom.
And for the most part we vouchsafe our friends,
Our lovers too, only such few clear notes
As we shall deem them likely to admire:
'Praise me for this' we say, or 'laugh at this,'
Or 'marvel at my candor' . . . all the while
Withholding what's most precious to ourselves,—
Some sinister depth of lust or fear or hatred,
The sombre note that gives the chord its power;
Or a white loveliness—if such we know—
Too much like fire to speak of without shame.

Well, this being so, and we who know it being
So curious about those well-locked houses,
The minds of those we know,—to enter softly,
And steal from floor to floor up shadowy stairways,
From room to quiet room, from wall to wall,
Breathing deliberately the very air,
Pressing our hands and nerves against warm darkness
To learn what ghosts are there,—
Suppose for once I set my doors wide open
And bid you in . . . Suppose I try to tell you
The secrets of this house, and how I live here;
Suppose I tell you who I am, in fact,
Deceiving you—as far as I may know it—
Only so much as I deceive myself.

4

If you are clever you already see me
As one who moves forever in a cloud
Of warm bright vanity: a luminous cloud
Which falls on all things with a quivering magic,
Changing such outlines as a light may change,
Brightening what lies dark to me, concealing
Those things that will not change . . . I walk sustained
In a world of things that flatter me: a sky
Just as I would have had it; trees and grass
Just as I would have shaped and colored them;
Pigeons and clouds and sun and whirling shadows,
And stars that brightening climb through mist at nightfall,—
In some deep way I am aware these praise me:
Where they are beautiful, or hint of beauty,
They point, somehow, to me. This water says,—
Shimmering at the sky, or undulating
In broken gleaming parodies of clouds,
Rippled in blue, or sending from cool depths
To meet the falling leaf the leaf's clear image,—
This water says, there is some secret in you
Akin to my clear beauty, beauty swaying
To mirror beauty, silently responsive
To all that circles you. This bare tree says,—
Austere and stark and leafless, split with frost,
Resonant in the wind, with rigid branches
Flung out against the sky,—this tall tree says,
There is some cold austerity in you,
A frozen strength, with long roots gnarled on rocks,
Fertile and deep; you bide your time, are patient,
Serene in silence, bare to outward seeming,
Concealing what reserves of power and beauty!
What teeming Aprils!—chorus of leaves on leaves!
These houses say, such walls in walls as ours,
Such streets of walls, solid and smooth of surface,
Such hills and cities of walls, walls upon walls;
Motionless in the sun, or dark with rain;
Walls pierced with windows, where the light may enter;
Walls windowless where darkness is desired;
Towers and labyrinths and domes and chambers,—
Amazing deep recesses, dark on dark,—
All these are like the walls which shape your spirit:

5

You move, are warm, within them, laugh within them,
Proud of their depth and strength; or sally from them,
To blow your Roland's horn against the world.
This deep cool room, with shadowed walls and ceiling,
Tranquil and cloistral, fragrant of my mind,
This cool room says,—just such a room have you,
It waits you always at the tops of stairways,
Withdrawn, remote, familiar to your uses,
Where you may cease pretence and be yourself.
And this embroidery, hanging on this wall,
Hung there forever,—these so soundless glidings
Of dragons golden-scaled, sheer birds of azure,
Coilings of leaves in pale vermilion, griffins
Drawing their rainbow wings through involutions
Of mauve chrysanthemums and lotus flowers,—
This goblin wood where someone cries enchantment,—
This says, just such an involuted beauty
Of thought and coiling thought, dream linked with dream,
Image to image gliding, wreathing lights,
Soundlessly cries enchantment in your mind:
You need but sit and close your eyes a moment
To see these rich designs unfold themselves.

And so, all things discern me, name me, praise me—
I walk in a world of silent voices, praising;
And in this world you see me like a wraith
Blown softly here and there, on silent winds.
'Praise me'—I say; and look, not in a glass,
But in your eyes, to see my image there—
Or in your mind; you smile, I am contented;
You look at me, with interest unfeigned,
And listen—I am pleased; or else, alone,
I watch thin bubbles veering brightly upward
From unknown depths,—my silver thoughts ascending;
Saying now this, now that, hinting of all things,—
Dreams, and desires, half-wishes, half-regrets,
Faint ghosts of memory, strange recognitions,—
But all with one deep meaning: this is I,
This is the glistening secret holy I,
This silver-wingèd wonder, insubstantial,
This singing ghost . . . And hearing, I am warmed.

6

You see me moving, then, as one who moves
Forever at the centre of his circle:
A circle filled with light. And into it
Come bulging shapes from darkness, loom gigantic,
Or huddle in dark again. A clock ticks clearly,
A gas-jet steadily whirs, light streams across me;
Two church bells, with alternate beat, strike nine;
And through these things my pencil pushes softly
To weave grey webs of lines on this clear page.
Snow falls and melts; the eaves make liquid music;
Black wheel-tracks line the snow-touched street; I turn
And look one instant at the half-dark gardens,
Where skeleton elm-trees reach with frozen gesture
Above unsteady lamps,—the black boughs lifted
Against a luminous snow-filled grey-gold sky.
'Beauty!' I cry. My feet move on, and take me
Between dark walls, with orange squares for windows.
Beauty; beheld like someone half-forgotten,
Remembered, with slow pang, as one neglected.
Well, I am frustrate; life has beaten me,
The thing I strongly seized has turned to darkness,
And darkness takes my heart . . . These skeleton elm-trees—
Leaning against that grey-gold snow-filled sky—
Beauty! they say, and at the edge of darkness
Extend vain arms in a frozen gesture of protest.
Voices are raised, a door is slammed. The lovers,
Murmuring in an adjacent room, grow silent,
The eaves make liquid music. Hours have passed,
And nothing changes, and everything is changed.
Exultation is dead, Beauty is harlot,—
And walks the streets: the thing I strongly seized,
Has turned to darkness, and darkness takes my heart.

If you could solve this darkness you would have me.
This causeless melancholy that comes with rain,
Or on such days as this, when large wet snowflakes
Drop heavily, with rain . . . whence rises this?
Well, so-and-so, this morning when I saw him,
Seemed much preoccupied, and would not smile;
And you, I saw too much; and you, too little;
And the word I chose for you, the golden word,

The word that should have struck so deep in purpose,
And set so many doors of wish wide open,
You let it fall, and would not stoop for it,
And smiled at me, and would not let me guess
Whether you saw it fall . . . These things, together,
With other things, still slighter, wove to magic,
And this in turn drew up dark memories;
And there I stand. This magic breaks and bleeds me,
Turning all frustrate dreams to chords and discords,—
Faces, and griefs, and words, and sunlit evenings,
And chains, self-forged, that will not break nor lengthen,
And cries that none can answer, few will hear.
Have these words meaning? Or would you see more clearly
If I should say 'My second wife grows tedious,
Or, like gay tulip, keeps no perfumed secret'?
Or 'one day dies eventless as another,
Leaving the seeker still unsatisfied,
And more convinced life yields no satisfaction'?
Or 'seek too hard, the eyes at length grow sightless,
And beauty shines in vain'?—

                              These things you ask for,
These you shall have . . . So, talking with my first wife,
At the dark end of evening, when she leaned
And smiled at me, her blue eyes weaving webs
Of finest fire, revolving me in scarlet,—
Calling to mind remote and small successions
Of countless other evenings ending so,—
I smiled, and met her kiss, and wished her dead;
Dead of a sudden sickness, or by my hands
Savagely killed; I saw her in her coffin,
I saw the coffin borne downstairs with trouble,
I saw myself alone there, palely watching,
Wearing a masque of grief so deeply acted
That grief itself possessed me. Time would pass,
And I would meet this girl,—my second wife—
And drop the masque of grief for one of passion.
Forward we move to meet, half hesitating,
We drown in each other's eyes, we laugh, we talk,
Looking now here, now there, and both pretending
We do not hear the powerful prelude begin

To throb beneath our words . . . The time approaches.
We lean unbalanced. The mute last glance between us,
Profoundly searching, opening, asking, yielding,
Is steadily met: our two lives draw together . . .
. . . 'What are you thinking of?' . . . My first wife's voice
Scattered these ghosts. 'Oh nothing—nothing much—
Just wondering where we'd be two years from now,
And what we might be doing . . .' And then remorse
Turned sharply in my mind to sudden pity,
And pity to acted passion. And one more evening
Drew to the usual end of sleep and silence.

And, as it is with this, so too with all things.
The pages of our lives are blurred palimpsest:
New lines are wreathed on old lines half-erased,
And those on older still; and so forever.
The old shines through the new, and colors it.
What's new? What's old? All things have double meanings,—
All things recur. I write a line, delighted,
(Or touch a woman's hand, or plumb a doctrine)
Only to find the same thing, known before,—
Only to find the same thing comes to-morrow.
This curious riddled dream I dreamed last night,—
Six years ago I dreamed it just as now;
The same man stooped to me; we rose from bondage,
And broke the accustomed order of our days,
And struck for the morning world, and light, and freedom.
What does it mean? Why is this hint repeated?
What anguish does it spring from, seek to end?

You see me, then, pass up and down these stairways,
Now through a beam of light, and now through shadow,—
Pursuing silent aims. No rest there is,—
No more for me than you. I move here always,
From quiet room to room, from wall to wall,
Searching and plotting, weaving a web of will.
This is my house, and now, perhaps, you know me.
Yet I confess, for all my best intentions,
Once more I have deceived you . . . I withhold
The one thing precious, the one dark wound that guides me;
And I have spread two snares for you, of lies.

9

No, I Shall Not Say

No, I shall not say why it is that I love you—
Why do you ask me, save for vanity?
Surely you would not have me, like a mirror,
Say 'yes,—your hair curls darkly back from the temples,
Your eyes are April grey . . . with jonquils in them'?
No, if I tell at all, I shall tell in silence.
I'll say—my childhood broke through chords of music
—Or were they chords of sun?—wherein fell shadows,
Or silences; I rose through waves of sunlight;
Or sometimes found an angel stooped above me
With wings of death, and a brow of cold clear beauty.
I lay in the warm sweet grass on a blue May morning,
My chin in a dandelion, my hands in clover,
And drowsed there like a bee. Blue days behind me
Reached like a chain of deep blue pools of magic,
Enchanted, silent, timeless. Days before me
Murmured of blue-sea mornings, noons of gold,
Green evenings streaked with lilac, bee-starred nights.
Confused soft clouds of foresight fled above me.
Sharp shafts of insight dazzled my eyes and pierced me.
I ran and turned and spun and danced in the sunlight,
Shrank, sometimes, from the freezing silence of Number,
Or crept once more to the warm white cave of sleep.

No, I shall not say 'this is why I praise you—
Because you say such wise things, or such foolish!'
You would not have me plead what you know better?
Let me instead be silent, only thinking—:
My childhood lives in me—or half-lives, rather—
And, if I close my eyes cool chords of logic
Flow up to me, long chords of wind and sunlight,
Shadows of intricate vines on sunlit walls,
Deep bells beating, with aeons of blue between them,

Grass blades leagues apart with worlds between them,
Walls thrust up to heaven with stars upon them.
I lay in my bed, and through the tall night window
Saw the green lightning lancing among the clouds,
And heard the harsh rain claw at the panes and roof.
How should I know—how should I now remember—
What half-dreamed God's wing curved above me?
What wings like swords? What eyes with the dread night in
   them?

This I shall say.—I lay by the hot white sand-dunes.
Small yellow flowers, sapless and squat and spiny,
Stared at the sky. And silently there above me,
Day after day, beyond all dreams or knowledge,
Presences swept, and over me streamed their shadows,
Swift and blue, or dark. What did they mean?
What sinister threat of power? What hint of weakness?
Prelude to what gigantic music, or subtle?
Only, I know, these shapes leaned over me,
Brooded upon me, paused, went flowing softly,
Glided and passed. I loved, I desired, I hated,
I struggled, I yielded and loved, was warmed to blossom.
You, when your eyes have evening sunlight in them,
Set these dunes before me, these salt bright flowers,
These presences. I drowse, they stream above me,
I struggle, I yield and love, I become that child.
You are the window (if I could tell I'd tell you)
Through which I see a clear far world of sunlight.
You are the silence (if you could hear you'd hear me)
In which I remember a thin still whisper of singing.
It is not you I laugh for, you I touch!
My hands, that touch you, suddenly touch a cobweb,
Coldly silvered, heavily silvered with dewdrops,
And clover, heavy with rain, in cold green grass.

Senlin: A Biography

I. HIS DARK ORIGINS

1

Senlin sits before us, and we see him.
He smokes his pipe before us, and we hear him.
Is he small, with reddish hair,
Does he light his pipe with a meditative stare,
And a pointed flame reflected in both eyes?
Is he sad and happy and foolish and wise?
Did no one see him enter the doors of the city,
Looking about him at roofs and trees and skies?
'I stepped from a cloud,' he says, 'as evening fell;
I walked on the sound of a bell;
I ran with winged heels along a gust;
Or is it true that I laughed and sprang from dust? . . .
Has no one, in a great autumnal forest,
When the wind bares the trees,
Heard the sad horn of Senlin slowly blown?
Has no one, on a mountain in the spring,
Heard Senlin sing?
Perhaps I came alone on a snow-white horse,—
Riding alone from the deep-starred night.
Perhaps I came on a ship whose sails were music,—
Sailing from moon or sun on a river of light.'

He lights his pipe with a pointed flame.
'Yet, there were many autumns before I came,
And many springs. And more will come, long after
There is no horn from me, or song, or laughter.'

The city dissolves about us, and its walls
Become an ancient forest. There is no sound

Except where an old twig tires and falls;
Or a lizard among the dead leaves crawls;
Or a flutter is heard in darkness along the ground.

Has Senlin become a forest? Do we walk in Senlin?
Is Senlin the wood we walk in,—ourselves,—the world?
Senlin! we cry . . . Senlin! again . . . No answer,
Only soft broken echoes backward whirled . . .

Yet we would say: this is no wood at all,
But a small white room with a lamp upon the wall;
And Senlin, before us, pale, with reddish hair,
Lights his pipe with a meditative stare.

2

Senlin, walking beside us, swings his arms
And turns his head to look at walls and trees.
The wind comes whistling from shrill stars of winter,
The lights are jewels, black roots freeze.
'Did I, then, stretch from the bitter earth like these,
Reaching upward with slow and rigid pain
To seek, in another air, myself again?'

(Immense and solitary in a desert of rocks
Behold a bewildered oak
With white clouds screaming through its leafy brain.)
'Or was I the single ant, or tinier thing,
That crept from the rocks of buried time
And dedicated its holy life to climb
From atom to beetling atom, jagged grain to grain,
Patiently out of the darkness we call sleep
Into the hollow gigantic world of light
Thinking the sky to be its destined shell,
Hoping to fit it well!—'

The city dissolves about us; and its walls
Are mountains of rock cruelly carved by wind.
Sand streams down their wasting sides, sand
Mounts upward slowly about them: foot and hand
We crawl and bleed among them! Is this Senlin?

In the desert of Senlin must we live and die?
We hear the decay of rocks, the crash of boulders,
Snarling of sand on sand. 'Senlin!' we cry.
'Senlin!' again . . . Our shadows revolve in silence
Under the soulless brilliance of blue sky.

Yet we would say: these are no rocks at all,
Nor desert of sand . . . here by a city wall
White lights jewel the evening, black roots freeze,
And Senlin turns his head to look at trees.

3

It is evening, Senlin says, and in the evening,
By a silent shore, by a far distant sea,
White unicorns come gravely down to the water.
In the lilac dusk they come, they are white and stately,
Stars hang over the purple waveless sea;
A sea on which no sail was ever lifted,
Where a human voice was never heard.
The shadows of vague hills are dark on the water,
The silent stars seem silently to sing.
And gravely come white unicorns down to the water,
One by one they come and drink their fill;
And daisies burn like stars on the darkened hill.

It is evening Senlin says, and in the evening
The leaves on the trees, abandoned by the light,
Look to the earth, and whisper, and are still.
The bat with horned wings, tumbling through the darkness,
Breaks the web, and the spider falls to the ground.
The starry dewdrop gathers upon the oakleaf,
Clings to the edge, and falls without a sound.
Do maidens spread their white palms to the starlight
And walk three steps to the east and clearly sing?
Do dewdrops fall like a shower of stars from willows?
Has the small moon a ghostly ring? . . .
White skeletons dance on the moonlit grass,
Singing maidens are buried in deep graves,
The stars hang over a sea like polished glass . . .
And solemnly one by one in the darkness there

Neighing far off on the haunted air
White unicorns come gravely down to the water.

No silver bells are heard. The westering moon
Lights the pale floors of caverns by the sea.
Wet weed hangs on the rock. In shimmering pools
Left on the rocks by the receding sea
Starfish slowly turn their white and brown
Or writhe on the naked rocks and drown.
Do sea-girls haunt these caves—do we hear faint singing?
Do we hear from under the sea a thin bell ringing?
Was that a white hand lifted among the bubbles
And fallen softly back?
No, these shores and caverns all are silent,
Dead in the moonlight; only, far above,
On the smooth contours of these headlands,
White amid the eternal black,
One by one in the moonlight there
Neighing far off on the haunted air
The unicorns come down to the sea.

4

Senlin, walking before us in the sunlight,
Bending his long legs in a peculiar way,
Goes to his work with thoughts of the universe.
His hands are in his pockets, he smokes his pipe,
He is happily conscious of roofs and skies;
And, without turning his head, he turns his eyes
To regard white horses drawing a small white hearse.
The sky is brilliant between the roofs,
The windows flash in the yellow sun,
On the hard pavement ring the hoofs,
The light wheels softly run.
Bright particles of sunlight fall,
Quiver and flash, gyrate and burn,
Honey-like heat flows down the wall,
The white spokes dazzle and turn.

Senlin, walking before us in the sunlight,
Regards the hearse with an introspective eye.

'Is it my childhood there,' he asks,
'Sealed in a hearse and hurrying by?'
He taps his trowel against a stone;
The trowel sings with a silver tone.

'Nevertheless, I know this well.
Bury it deep and toll a bell,
Bury it under land or sea,
You cannot bury it save in me.'

It is as if his soul had become a city,
With noisily peopled streets, and through these streets
Senlin himself comes driving a small white hearse . . .
'Senlin!' we cry. He does not turn his head.
But is that Senlin?—or is this city Senlin,—
Quietly watching the burial of its dead?
Dumbly observing the cortège of its dead?
Yet we would say that all this is but madness:
Around a distant corner trots the hearse.
And Senlin walks before us in the sunlight
Happily conscious of his universe.

5

In the hot noon, in an old and savage garden,
The peach-tree grows. Its ugly cruel roots
Rend and rifle the silent earth for moisture.
Above, in the blue, hang warm and golden fruits.
Look, how the cancerous roots crack mould and stone!
Earth, if she had a voice, would wail her pain.
Is she the victim? Or is the tree the victim?
Delicate blossoms opened in the rain,
Black bees flew among them in the sunlight,
And sacked them ruthlessly; and now a bird
Hangs, sharp-eyed, in the leaves, and pecks the fruit;
And the peach-tree dreams, and does not say a word.
. . . Senlin, tapping his trowel against a stone,
Observes this tree he planted: it is his own.

'You will think it strange,' says Senlin, 'but this tree
Utters profound things in this garden;

And in it silence speaks to me.
I have sensations, when I stand beneath it,
As if its leaves looked at me, and could see;
And these thin leaves, even in windless air,
Seem to be whispering me a choral music,
Insubstantial but debonair.

"Regard," they seem to say,
"Our idiot root, which going its brutal way
Has cracked your garden wall!
Ugly, is it not?
A desecration of this place . . .
And yet, without it, could we exist at all?"
Thus, rustling with importance, they seem to me
To make their apology;
Yet, while they apologize,
Ask me a wary question with their eyes.
Yes, it is true their origin is low—
Brutish and dull and cruel . . . and it is true
Their roots have cracked the wall. But do we know
The leaves less cruel—the root less beautiful?
Sometimes it seems as if there grew
In the dull garden of my mind
A tree like this, which, singing with delicate leaves,
Yet cracks the walls with cruel roots and blind.
Sometimes, indeed, it appears to me
That I myself am such a tree . . .'

. . . And as we hear from Senlin these strange words
So, slowly, in the sunlight, he becomes this tree:
And among the pleasant leaves hang sharp-eyed birds
While cruel roots dig downward secretly.

6

Rustling among his odds and ends of knowledge
Suddenly, to his wonder, Senlin finds
How Cleopatra and Senebtisi
Were dug by many hands from ancient tombs.
Cloth after scented cloth the sage unwinds:

Delicious, to see our futile modern sunlight
Dance like a harlot among these Dogs and Dooms!

First, the huge pyramid, with rock on rock
Bloodily piled to heaven; and under this
A gilded cavern, bat-festooned;
And here in rows on rows, with gods about them,
Cloudily lustrous, dim, the sacred coffins,
Silver-starred and crimson-mooned.

What holy secret shall we now uncover?
Inside the outer coffin is a second;
Inside the second, smaller, lies a third.
This one is carved, and like a human body;
And painted over with fish and bull and bird.
Here are men walking stiffly in procession,
Blowing horns or lifting spears.
Where do they march to? Where do they come from?
Soft whine of horns is in our ears.

Inside, the third, a fourth . . . and this the artist,—
A priest, perhaps?—did most to make resemble
The flesh of her who lies within.
The brown eyes widely stare at the bat-hung ceiling.
The hair is black, the mouth is thin.

Princess! Secret of life! We come to praise you!
The torch is lowered, this coffin too we open,
And the dark air is drunk with musk and myrrh.
Here are the thousand white and scented wrappings,
The gilded mask, and jewelled eyes, of her.

And now the body itself, brown, gaunt, and ugly,
And the hollow skull, in which the brains are withered,
Lie bare before us. Princess, is this all?
Something there was we asked that is not answered.
Soft bats, in rows, hang on the lustred wall.

And all we hear is a whisper sound of music,
Of brass horns dustily raised and briefly blown,
And a cry of grief; and men in a stiff procession
Marching away and softly gone.

7

'And am I then, a pyramid?' says Senlin,
'In which are caves and coffins, where lies hidden
Some old and mocking hieroglyph of flesh?
Or am I rather the moonlight, spreading subtly
Above those stones and times?
Or the green blade of grass that bravely grows
Between two massive boulders of black basalt
Year after year, and fades and blows?'

Senlin, sitting before us in the lamplight,
Laughs, and lights his pipe. The yellow flame
Minutely flares in his eyes, minutely dwindles.
Does a blade of grass have Senlin for a name?
Yet we would say that we have seen him somewhere,
A tiny spear of green beneath the blue,
Playing his destiny in a sun-warmed crevice
With the gigantic fates of frost and dew.

Does a spider come and spin his gossamer ladder
Rung by silver rung
Chaining it fast to Senlin? Its faint shadow
Flung, waveringly, where his is flung?
Does a raindrop dazzle starlike down his length
Trying his futile strength?
A snowflake startle him? The stars defeat him?
Through aeons of dusk have birds above him sung?
Time is a wind, says Senlin; time, like music,
Blows over us its mournful beauty, passes,
And leaves behind a shadowy recollection,—
A helpless gesture of mist above the grasses.

8

In cold blue lucid dusk before the sunrise,
One yellow star sings over a peak of snow,
And melts and vanishes in a light like roses.
Through slanting mist, black rocks appear and glow.

The clouds flow downward, slowly as grey glaciers,
Or up to pale rose-azure pass.
Blue streams tinkle down from snow to boulders,
From boulders to white grass.

Icicles on the pine tree melt
And softly flash in the sun:
In long straight lines the star-drops fall
One by one.

Is a voice heard while the shadows still are long,
Borne slowly down on the sparkled air?
Is a thin bell heard from the peak of silence?
Is someone among the high snows there?

Where the blue stream flows coldly among the meadows
And mist still clings to rock and tree
Senlin walks alone; and from that twilight
Looks darkly up, to see

The calm unmoving peak of snow-white silence,
The rocks aflame with ice, the rose-blue sky . . .
Ghost-like, a cloud descends from twinkling ledges,
To nod before the dwindling sun and die.

'Something there is,' says Senlin, 'in that mountain,
Something forgotten now, that once I knew . . .'
We walk before a sun-tipped peak in silence,
Our shadows descend before us, long and blue.

II. HIS FUTILE PREOCCUPATIONS

1

I am a house, says Senlin, locked and darkened,
Sealed from the sun with wall and door and blind.
Summon me loudly, and you'll hear slow footsteps
Ring far and faint in the galleries of my mind.
You'll hear soft steps on an old and dusty stairway;
Peer darkly through some corner of a pane,

You'll see me with a faint light coming slowly,
Pausing above some balcony of the brain . . .

I am a city . . . In the blue light of evening
Wind wanders among my streets and makes them fair;
I am a room of rock . . . a maiden dances
Lifting her hands, tossing her golden hair.
She combs her hair, the room of rock is darkened,
She extends herself in me, and I am sleep.
It is my pride that starlight is above me;
I dream amid waves of air, my walls are deep.

I am a door . . . before me roils the darkness,
Behind me ring clear waves of sound and light.
Stand in the shadowy street outside, and listen—
The crying of violins assails the night . . .
My walls are deep, but the cries of music pierce them;
They shake with the sound of drums . . . yet it is strange
That I should know so little what means this music,
Hearing it always within me change and change.

Knock on the door,—and you shall have an answer.
Open the heavy walls to set me free,
And blow a horn to call me into the sunlight,—
And startled, then, what a strange thing you shall see!
Nuns, murderers, and drunkards, saints and sinners,
Lover and dancing girl and sage and clown
Will laugh upon you, and you will find me nowhere.
I am a room, a house, a street, a town.

2

It is morning, Senlin says, and in the morning
When the light drips through the shutters like the dew,
I arise, I face the sunrise,
And do the things my fathers learned to do.
Stars in the purple dusk above the rooftops
Pale in a saffron mist and seem to die,
And I myself on a swiftly tilting planet
Stand before a glass and tie my tie.

Vine leaves tap my window,
Dew-drops sing to the garden stones,
The robin chirps in the chinaberry tree
Repeating three clear tones.

It is morning. I stand by the mirror
And tie my tie once more.
While waves far off in a pale rose twilight
Crash on a coral shore.
I stand by a mirror and comb my hair:
How small and white my face!—
The green earth tilts through a sphere of air
And bathes in a flame of space.

There are houses hanging above the stars
And stars hung under a sea.
And a sun far off in a shell of silence
Dapples my walls for me.

It is morning, Senlin says, and in the morning
Should I not pause in the light to remember god?
Upright and firm I stand on a star unstable,
He is immense and lonely as a cloud.
I will dedicate this moment before my mirror
To him alone, for him I will comb my hair.
Accept these humble offerings, cloud of silence!
I will think of you as I descend the stair.

Vine leaves tap my window,
The snail-track shines on the stones,
Dew-drops flash from the chinaberry tree
Repeating two clear tones.

It is morning, I awake from a bed of silence,
Shining I rise from the starless waters of sleep.
The walls are about me still as in the evening,
I am the same, and the same name still I keep.
The earth revolves with me, yet makes no motion,
The stars pale silently in a coral sky.
In a whistling void I stand before my mirror,
Unconcerned, and tie my tie.

There are horses neighing on far-off hills
Tossing their long white manes,
And mountains flash in the rose-white dusk,
Their shoulders black with rains.
It is morning. I stand by the mirror
And surprise my soul once more;
The blue air rushes above my ceiling,
There are suns beneath my floor.

. . . It is morning, Senlin says, I ascend from darkness
And depart on the winds of space for I know not where,
My watch is wound, a key is in my pocket,
And the sky is darkened as I descend the stair.
There are shadows across the windows, clouds in heaven,
And a god among the stars; and I will go
Thinking of him as I might think of daybreak
And humming a tune I know.

Vine leaves tap at the window,
Dew-drops sing to the garden stones,
The robin chirps in the chinaberry tree
Repeating three clear tones.

3
I walk to my work, says Senlin, along a street
Superbly hung in space.
I lift these mortal stones, and with my trowel
I tap them into place.
But is god, perhaps, a giant who ties his tie
Grimacing before a colossal glass of sky?

These stones are heavy, these stones decay,
These stones are wet with rain,
I build them into a wall today,
Tomorrow they fall again.

Does god arise from a chaos of starless sleep,
Rise from the dark and stretch his arms and yawn;
And drowsily look from the window at his garden;
And rejoice at the dewdrop sparkling on his lawn?

Does he remember, suddenly, with amazement,
The yesterday he left in sleep,—his name,—
Or the glittering street superbly hung in wind
Along which, in the dusk, he slowly came?

I devise new patterns for laying stones
And build a stronger wall.
One drop of rain astonishes me
And I let my trowel fall.

The flashing of leaves delights my eyes,
Blue air delights my face;
I will dedicate this stone to god
As I tap it into its place.

4

That woman—did she try to attract my attention?
Is it true I saw her smile and nod?
She turned her head and smiled . . . was it for me?
It is better to think of work or god.
The clouds pile coldly above the houses
Slow wind revolves the leaves:
It begins to rain, and the first long drops
Are slantingly blown from eaves.

But it is true she tried to attract my attention!
She pressed a rose to her chin and smiled.
Her hand was white by the richness of her hair,
Her eyes were those of a child.
It is true she looked at me as if she liked me,
And turned away, afraid to look too long!
She watched me out of the corners of her eyes;
And, tapping time with fingers, hummed a song.

. . . Nevertheless, I will think of work,
With a trowel in my hands;
Or the vague god who blows like clouds
Above these dripping lands . . .

But . . . is it sure she tried to attract my attention?
She leaned her elbow in a peculiar way
There in the crowded room . . . she touched my hand . . .
She must have known, and yet,—she let it stay.
Music of flesh! Music of root and sod!
Leaf touching leaf in the rain!
Impalpable clouds of red ascend,
Red clouds blow over my brain.

Did she await from me some sign of acceptance?
I smoothed my hair with a faltering hand.
I started a feeble smile, but the smile was frozen:
Perhaps, I thought, I misunderstand.
Is it to be conceived that I could attract her—
This dull and futile flesh attract such fire?
I,—with a trowel's dulness in hand and brain!—
Take on some godlike aspect, rouse desire?
Incredible! . . . delicious! . . . I will wear
A brighter color of tie, arranged with care;
I will delight in god as I comb my hair.

And the conquests of my bolder past return
Like strains of music, some lost tune
Recalled from youth and a happier time.
I take my sweetheart's arm in the dusk once more;
Once more we climb

Up the forbidden stairway,
Under the flickering light, along the railing:
I catch her hand in the dark, we laugh once more,
I hear the rustle of silk, and follow swiftly,
And softly at last we close the door.

Yes, it is true that woman tried to attract me:
It is true she came out of time for me,
Came from the swirling and savage forest of earth,
The cruel eternity of the sea.
She parted the leaves of waves and rose from silence
Shining with secrets she did not know.
Music of dust! Music of web and web!
And I, bewildered, let her go.

I light my pipe. The flame is yellow,
Edged underneath with blue.
These thoughts are truer of god, perhaps,
Than thoughts of god are true.

5

It is noontime, Senlin says, and a street piano
Strikes sharply against the sunshine a harsh chord,
And the universe is suddenly agitated,
And pain to my heart goes glittering like a sword.
Do I imagine it? The dust is shaken,
The sunlight quivers, the brittle oak-leaves tremble.
The world, disturbed, conceals its agitation;
And I, too, will dissemble.

Yet it is sorrow has found my heart,
Sorrow for beauty, sorrow for death;
And pain twirls slowly among the trees.

The street-piano revolves its glittering music,
The sharp notes flash and dazzle and turn,
Memory's knives are in this sunlit silence,
They ripple and lazily burn.
The star on which my shadow falls is frightened,—
It does not move; my trowel taps a stone,
The sweet note wavers amid derisive music;
And I, in a horror of sunlight, stand alone.

Do not recall my weakness, savage music!
Let the knives rest!
Impersonal, harsh, the music revolves and glitters,
And the notes like poniards pierce my breast.
And I remember the shadows of webs on stones,
And the sound of rain on withered grass,
And a sorrowful face that looked without illusions
At its image in the glass.

Do not recall my childhood, pitiless music!
The green blades flicker and gleam,

The red bee bends the clover, deeply humming;
In the blue sea above me lazily stream
Cloud upon thin-blown cloud, revolving, scattering;
The mulberry tree rakes heaven and drops its fruit;
Amazing sunlight sings in the opened vault
On dust and bones; and I am mute.

It is noon; the bells let fall soft flowers of sound.
They turn on the air, they shrink in the flare of noon.
It is night; and I lie alone, and watch through the window
The terrible ice-white emptiness of the moon.
Small bells, far off, spill jewels of sound like rain,
A long wind hurries them whirled and far,
A cloud creeps over the moon, my bed is darkened,
I hold my breath and watch a star.

Do not disturb my memories, heartless music!
I stand once more by a vine-dark moonlit wall,
The sound of my footsteps dies in a void of moonlight,
And I watch white jasmine fall.
Is it my heart that falls? Does earth itself
Drift, a white petal, down the sky?
One bell-note goes to the stars in the blue-white silence,
Solitary and mournful, a somnolent cry.

6

Death himself in the rain . . . death himself . . .
Death in the savage sunlight . . . skeletal death . . .
I hear the clack of his feet,
Clearly on stones, softly in dust;
He hurries among the trees
Whirling the leaves, tossing his hands from waves.
Listen! the immortal footsteps beat!

Death himself in the grass, death himself,
Gyrating invisibly in the sun,
Scatters the grass-blades, whips the wind,
Tears at boughs with malignant laughter:
On the long echoing air I hear him run.

Death himself in the dusk, gathering lilacs,
Breaking a white-fleshed bough,
Strewing purple on a cobwebbed lawn,
Dancing, dancing,
The long red sun-rays glancing
On flailing arms, skipping with hideous knees,
Cavorting grotesque ecstasies:
I do not see him, but I see the lilacs fall,
I hear the scrape of knuckles against the wall,
The leaves are tossed and tremble where he plunges among them,
And I hear the sound of his breath,
Sharp and whistling, the rhythm of death.

It is evening: the lights on a long street balance and sway.
In the purple ether they swing and silently sing,
The street is a gossamer swung in space,
And death himself in the wind comes dancing along it,
And the lights, like raindrops, tremble and swing.
Hurry, spider, and spread your glistening web,
For death approaches!
Hurry, rose, and open your heart to the bee,
For death approaches!
Maiden, let down your hair for the hands of your lover,
Comb it with moonlight and wreathe it with leaves,
For death approaches!

Death, huge in the star; small in the sand-grain;
Death himself in the rain,
Drawing the rain about him like a garment of jewels:
I hear the sound of his feet
On the stairs of the wind, in the sun,
In the forests of the sea . . .
Listen! the immortal footsteps beat!

7

It is noontime, Senlin says. The sky is brilliant
Above a green and dreaming hill.
I lay my trowel down. The pool is cloudless,
The grass, the wall, the peach-tree, all are still.

It appears to me that I am one with these:
A hill, upon whose back are a wall and trees.
It is noontime: all seems still
Upon this green and flowering hill.

Yet suddenly, out of nowhere in the sky,
A cloud comes whirling, and flings
A lazily coiling vortex of shade on the hill.
It crosses the hill, and a bird in the peach-tree sings.
Amazing! Is there a change?
The hill seems somehow strange.
It is noontime. And in the tree
The leaves are delicately disturbed
Where the bird descends invisibly.
It is noontime. And in the pool
The sky is blue and cool.

Yet suddenly, out of nowhere,
Something flings itself at the hill,
Tears with claws at the earth,
Lunges and hisses and softly recoils,
Crashing against the green.
The peach-tree braces itself, the pool is frightened,
The grass blades quiver, the bird is still;
The wall silently struggles against the sunlight;
A terror stiffens the hill.
The trees turn rigidly, to face
Something that circles with slow pace:
The blue pool seems to shrink
From something that slides above its brink.
What struggle is this, ferocious and still—
What war in sunlight on this hill?
What is it creeping to dart
Like a knife-blade at my heart?

It is noontime, Senlin says, and all is tranquil:
The brilliant sky burns over a greenbright earth.
The peach-tree dreams in the sun, the wall is contented.
A bird in the peach-leaves, moving from sun to shadow,
Phrases again his unremembering mirth,
His lazily beautiful, foolish, mechanical mirth.

8

The pale blue gloom of evening comes
Among the phantom forests and walls
With a mournful and rhythmic sound of drums.
My heart is disturbed with a sound of myriad throbbing,
Persuasive and sinister, near and far:
In the blue evening of my heart
I hear the thrum of the evening star.

My work is uncompleted; and yet I hurry,—
Hearing the whispered pulsing of those drums,—
To enter the luminous walls and woods of night.
It is the eternal mistress of the world
Who shakes these drums for my delight.
Listen! the drums of the leaves, the drums of the dust,
The delicious quivering of this air!

I will leave my work unfinished, and I will go
With ringing and certain step through the laughter of chaos
To the one small room in the void I know.
Yesterday it was there,—
Will I find it tonight once more when I climb the stair?
The drums of the street beat swift and soft:
In the blue evening of my heart
I hear the throb of the bridal star.
It weaves deliciously in my brain
A tyrannous melody of her:
Hands in sunlight, threads of rain
Against a weeping face that fades,
Snow on a blackened window-pane;
Fire, in a dusk of hair entangled;
Flesh, more delicate than fruit;
And a voice that searches quivering nerves
For a string to mute.

My life is uncompleted: and yet I hurry
Among the tinkling forests and walls of evening
To a certain fragrant room.
Who is it that dances there, to a beating of drums,

While stars on a grey sea bud and bloom?
She stands at the top of the stair,
With the lamplight on her hair.
I will walk through the snarling of streams of space
And climb the long steps carved from wind
And rise once more toward her face.
Listen! the drums of the drowsy trees
Beating our nuptial ecstasies!

Music spins from the heart of silence
And twirls me softly upon the air:
It takes my hand and whispers to me:
It draws the web of the moonlight down.
There are hands, it says, as cool as snow,
The hands of the Venus of the sea;
There are waves of sound in a mermaid-cave;—
Come—then—come with me!
The flesh of the sea-rose new and cool,
The wavering image of her who comes
At dusk by a blue sea-pool.

Whispers upon the haunted air—
Whisper of foam-white arm and thigh;
And a shower of delicate lights blown down
From the laughing sky! . . .
Music spins from a far-off room.
Do you remember,—it seems to say,—
The mouth that smiled, beneath your mouth,
And kissed you . . . yesterday?
It is your own flesh waits for you.
Come! you are incomplete! . . .
The drums of the universe once more
Morosely beat.
It is the harlot of the world
Who clashes the leaves like ghostly drums
And disturbs the solitude of my heart
As evening comes!

I leave my work once more, and walk
Along a street that sways in the wind.
I leave these stones, and walk once more

Along infinity's shore.
I climb the golden-laddered stair;
Among the stars in the void I climb:
I ascend the golden-laddered hair
Of the harlot-queen of time:
She laughs from a window in the sky,
Her white arms downward reach to me!
We are the universe that spins
In a dim ethereal sea.

9

It is evening, Senlin says, and in the evening
The throbbing of drums has languidly died away.
Forest and sea are still. We breathe in silence
And strive to say the things flesh cannot say.
The soulless wind falls slowly about the earth
And finds no rest.
The lover stares at the setting star,—the wakeful lover
Who finds no peace on his lover's breast.
The snare of desire that bound us in is broken;
Softly, in sorrow, we draw apart, and see,
Far off, the beauty we thought our flesh had captured,—
The star we longed to be but could not be.
Come back! We will laugh once more at the words we said!
We say them slowly again, but the words are dead.
Come back, beloved! . . . The blue void falls between,
We cry to each other: alone; unknown; unseen.

We are the grains of sand that run and rustle
In the dry wind,
We are the grains of sand who thought ourselves
Immortal.
You touch my hand, time bears you away,—
An alien star for whom I have no word.
What are the meaningless things you say?
I answer you, but am not heard.

It is evening, Senlin says;
And a dream in ruin falls.
Once more we turn in pain, bewildered,

Among our finite walls:
The walls we built ourselves with patient hands;
For the god who sealed a question in our flesh.

10

It is moonlight. Alone, in silence,
I ascend my stairs once more,
While waves, remote in a pale blue starlight,
Crash on a coral shore.
It is moonlight. The garden is silent.
I stand in my room alone.
Across my wall, from the far-off moon,
A spear of fire is thrown.

There are houses hanging above the stars,
And stars hung under a sea;
And a wind from the long blue vault of time
Waves my curtains for me.
I wait in the dark once more,
Hung between space and space;
Before the mirror I lift my hands
And face my remembered face.

Is it I who stand in a question here,
Asking to know my name?
It is I; yet I know not whither I go;
Nor why; nor whence I came.

It is I, who awoke at dawn
And arose and descended the stair;
Conceiving a god in the eye of the sun,—
In a woman's hands and hair.
It is I, whose flesh is grey with the stones
I builded into a wall:
With a mournful melody in my brain
Of a tune I cannot recall.

There are roses to break: and mouths to kiss;
And the phantom king of death.
I remember a rain-drop on a stone;

33

An eye in the hawthorn breath . . .
And the star I laugh on tilts through heaven;
And the heavens are black and steep.
I will forget these things once more
In the silence of sleep.

III. HIS CLOUDY DESTINY

1

Senlin sat before us and we heard him.
He smoked his pipe before us and we saw him.
Was he small, with reddish hair,
Did he light his pipe with a meditative stare
And a twinkling flame reflected in blue eyes?
'I am alone': said Senlin; 'in a forest of leaves
The single leaf that creeps and falls.
The single blade of grass in a desert of grass
That none foresaw and none recalls.
The single shell that a green wave shatters
In tiny specks of whiteness on brown sands . . .
How shall you understand me with your hearts,
Who cannot reach me with your hands? . . .'

The city dissolves about us, and its walls
Are the sands beside a sea.
We plunge in a chaos of dunes, white waves before us
Crash on kelp tumultuously,
Gulls wheel over the foam, the clouds blow tattered,
The sun is swallowed . . . Has Senlin become a shore?
Is Senlin a grain of sand beneath our footsteps,
A speck of shell upon which waves will roar? . . .
Senlin! we cry . . . Senlin! again . . . no answer,
Only the crash of sea on a shell-white shore.

Yet, we would say, this is no shore at all,
But a small bright room with lamplight on the wall;
And the familiar chair
Where Senlin sat, with lamplight on his hair.

2

Senlin, alone before us, played a music.
Was it himself he played? . . . We sat and listened,
Perplexed and pleased and tired.
'Listen!' he said, 'and you will learn a secret—
Though it is not the secret you desired.
I have not found a meaning that will praise you!
Out of the heart of silence comes this music,
Quietly speaks and dies.
Look! there is one white star above black houses!
And a tiny man who climbs towards the skies!
Where does he walk to? What does he leave behind him?
What was his foolish name?
What did he stop to say, before he left you
As simply as he came?
"Death?" did it sound like, "love, and god, and laughter,
Sunlight, and work, and pain . . . ?"
No—it appears to me that these were symbols
Of simple truths he found no way to explain.
He spoke, but found you could not understand him—
You were alone, and he was alone.

"He sought to touch you, and found he could not reach you,—
He sought to understand you, and could not hear you.
And so this music, which I play before you,—
Does it mean only what it seems to mean?
Or is it a dance of foolish waves in sunlight
Above a desperate depth of things unseen?
Listen! Do you not hear the singing voices
Out of the darkness of this sea?
But no: you cannot hear them; for if you heard them
You would have heard and captured me.
Yet I am here, talking of laughter.
Laughter and love and work and god;
As I shall talk of these same things hereafter
In wave and sod.
Walk on a hill and call me: "Senlin! . . . Senlin! . . ."
Will I not answer you as clearly as now?

35

Listen to rain, and you will hear me speaking.
Look for my heart in the breaking of a bough . . .'

3

Senlin stood before us in the sunlight,
And laughed, and walked away.
Did no one see him leaving the doors of the city,
Looking behind him as if he wished to stay?
Has no one, in the forests of the evening,
Heard the sad horn of Senlin slowly blown?
For somewhere, in the worlds-in-worlds about us,
He changes still, unfriended and alone.
Is he the star on which we walk at daybreak,
The light that blinds our eyes?
'Senlin!' we cry. 'Senlin!' again . . . no answer:
Only the soulless brilliance of blue skies.

Yet we would say, this was no man at all,
But a dream we dreamed, and vividly recall;
And we are mad to walk in wind and rain
Hoping to find, somewhere, that dream again.

Tetélestai

I

How shall we praise the magnificence of the dead,
The great man humbled, the haughty brought to dust?
Is there a horn we should not blow as proudly
For the meanest of us all, who creeps his days,
Guarding his heart from blows, to die obscurely?
I am no king, have laid no kingdoms waste,
Taken no princes captive, led no triumphs
Of weeping women through long walls of trumpets;
Say rather, I am no one, or an atom;
Say rather, two great gods, in a vault of starlight,

Play ponderingly at chess, and at the game's end
One of the pieces, shaken, falls to the floor
And runs to the darkest corner; and that piece
Forgotten there, left motionless, is I . . .
Say that I have no name, no gifts, no power,
Am only one of millions, mostly silent;
One who came with eyes and hands and a heart,
Looked on beauty, and loved it, and then left it.
Say that the fates of time and space obscured me,
Led me a thousand ways to pain, bemused me,
Wrapped me in ugliness; and like great spiders
Dispatched me at their leisure . . . Well, what then?
Should I not hear, as I lie down in dust,
The horns of glory blowing above my burial?

II

Morning and evening opened and closed above me:
Houses were built above me; trees let fall
Yellowing leaves upon me, hands of ghosts;
Rain has showered its arrows of silver upon me
Seeking my heart; winds have roared and tossed me;
Music in long blue waves of sound has borne me
A helpless weed to shores of unthought silence;
Time, above me, within me, crashed its gongs
Of terrible warning, sifting the dust of death;
And here I lie. Blow now your horns of glory
Harshly over my flesh, you trees, you waters!
You stars and suns, Canopus, Deneb, Rigel,
Let me, as I lie down, here in this dust,
Hear far off, your whispered salutation!
Roar now above my decaying flesh, you winds,
Whirl out your earth-scents over this body, tell me
Of ferns and stagnant pools, wild roses, hillsides!
Anoint me, rain, let crash your silver arrows
On this hard flesh! I am the one who named you,
I lived in you, and now I die in you.
I your son, your daughter, treader of music,
Lie broken, conquered . . . Let me not fall in silence.

III

I, the restless one; the circler of circles;
Herdsman and roper of stars, who could not capture
The secret of self; I who was tyrant to weaklings,
Striker of children; destroyer of women; corrupter
Of innocent dreamers, and laughter at beauty; I,
Too easily brought to tears and weakness by music,
Baffled and broken by love, the helpless beholder
Of the war in my heart of desire with desire, the struggle
Of hatred with love, terror with hunger; I
Who laughed without knowing the cause of my laughter, who grew
Without wishing to grow, a servant to my own body;
Loved without reason the laughter and flesh of a woman,
Enduring such torments to find her! I who at last
Grow weaker, struggle more feebly, relent in my purpose,
Choose for my triumph an easier end, look backward
At earlier conquests; or, caught in the web, cry out
In a sudden and empty despair, 'Tetélestai!'
Pity me, now! I, who was arrogant, beg you!
Tell me, as I lie down, that I was courageous.
Blow horns of victory now, as I reel and am vanquished.
Shatter the sky with trumpets above my grave.

IV

. . . Look! this flesh how it crumbles to dust and is blown!
These bones, how they grind in the granite of frost and are
     nothing!
This skull, how it yawns for a flicker of time in the darkness,
Yet laughs not and sees not! It is crushed by a hammer of
     sunlight,
And the hands are destroyed . . . Press down through the
     leaves of the jasmine,
Dig through the interlaced roots—nevermore will you find me;
I was no better than dust, yet you cannot replace me . . .
Take the soft dust in your hand—does it stir: does it sing?
Has it lips and a heart? Does it open its eyes to the sun?
Does it run, does it dream, does it burn with a secret, or tremble
In terror of death? Or ache with tremendous decisions? . . .

38

Listen! . . . It says: 'I lean by the river. The willows
Are yellowed with bud. White clouds roar up from the south
And darken the ripples; but they cannot darken my heart,
Nor the face like a star in my heart . . . Rain falls on the water
And pelts it, and rings it with silver. The willow trees glisten,
The sparrows chirp under the eaves; but the face in my heart
Is a secret of music . . . I wait in the rain and am silent.'
Listen again! . . . It says: 'I have worked, I am tired,
The pencil dulls in my hand: I see through the window
Walls upon walls of windows with faces behind them,
Smoke floating up to the sky, an ascension of sea-gulls.
I am tired. I have struggled in vain, my decision was fruitless,
Why then do I wait? with darkness, so easy, at hand! . . .
But tomorrow, perhaps . . . I will wait and endure till tomor-
    row!' . . .
Or again: 'It is dark. The decision is made. I am vanquished
By terror of life. The walls mount slowly about me
In coldness. I had not the courage. I was forsaken.
I cried out, was answered by silence . . . Tetélestai! . . .'

          V

Hear how it babbles!—Blow the dust out of your hand,
With its voices and visions, tread on it, forget it, turn homeward
With dreams in your brain . . . This, then, is the humble, the
    nameless,—
The lover, the husband and father, the struggler with shadows,
The one who went down under shoutings of chaos, the weakling
Who cried his 'forsaken!' like Christ on the darkening hilltop! . . .
This, then, is the one who implores, as he dwindles to silence,
A fanfare of glory . . . And which of us dares to deny him?

Psychomachia

Tent-caterpillars, as you see, (he said)
Have nested in these cherry-trees, and stripped
All sound of leaves from them. You see their webs
Like broken harp-strings, of a fairy kind,
Shine in the moonlight.

                    And then I to him:
But is this why, when all the houses sleep,
You meet me here,—to tell me only this,
That caterpillars weave their webs in trees?
This road I know. I have walked many times
These sandy ruts. I know these starveling trees,
Their gestures of stiff agony in winter,
And the sharp conscious pain that gnaws them now.
But there is mystery, a message learned,
A word flung down from nowhere, caught by you,
And hither brought for me. How shines that word,
From what star comes it? . . . This is what I seek.

And he in answer: Can you hear the blood
Cry out like jangled bells from all these twigs;
Or feel the ghosts of blossom touch your face?
Walk you amid these trees as one who walks
Upon a field where lie the newly slain
And those who darkly die? And hear you crying?
Flesh here is torn from flesh. The tongue's plucked out.
What speech then would you have, where speech is tongueless,
And nothing, nothing, but a welling up of pain?

I answered: You may say these smitten trees,
Being leafless, have no tongues and cannot speak.
How comforts that my question? . . . You have come,

I know, as you come always, with a meaning.
What, then, is in your darkness of hurt trees;
What bird, sequestered in that wilderness
Of inarticulate pain, wrong ill-endured,
And death not understood, but bides his time
To sing a piercing phrase? Why sings he not?
I am familiar, long, with pain and death,
Endure as all do, lift dumb eyes to question
Uncomprehended wounds; I have my forest
Of injured trees, whose bare twigs show the moon
Their shameful floating webs; and I have walked,
As now we walk, to listen there to bells
Of pain, bubbles of blood, and ached to feel
The ghosts of blossom pass. But is there not
The mystery, the fugitive shape that sings
A sudden beauty there that comes like peace?

You know this road, he said, and how it leads
Beyond starved trees to bare grey poverty grass;
Then lies the marsh beyond, and then the beach,
With dry curled waves of sea-weed, and the sea.
There, in the fog, you hear the row-locks thump,
And there you see the fisherman come in
From insubstantial nothing to a shore
As dim and insubstantial. He is old,
His boat is old and grey, the oars are worn.
You know this,—you have seen this?

                      And then I:
I know, have seen this, and have felt the shore
As dim and thin as mist; and I have wondered
That it upheld me, did not let me fall
Through nothing into nothing . . . And the oars,
Worn down like human nerves against the world;
And the worn road that leads to sleeping houses
And weeping trees. But is this all you say?
For there is mystery, a word you have
That shines within your mind. Now speak that word.

And he in answer: So you have the landscape
With all its nerves and voices. It is yours.

Do with it what you will. But never try
To go away from it, for that is death.
Dwell in it, know its houses, and cursed trees,
And call it sorrow. Is this not enough?
Love you not shameful webs? It is enough.
There is no need for bird, or sudden peace.

II

The plain no herbage had, but all was bare
And swollen livid sand in ridges heaped;
And in the sharp cold light that filled the east
Beneath one cloud that was a bird with wings
I saw a figure shape itself, as whirling
It took up sand and moved across the sand.
A man it was, and here and there he ran
Beating his arms, now falling, rising now,
Struggling, for so it seemed, against the air.
But, as I watched, the cloud that was a bird
Lifted its wings; and the white light intense
Poured down upon him. Then I saw him, naked,
Amid that waste, at war with a strange beast
Or monster, many-armed and ever-changing;
That now was like an octopus of air,
Now like a spider with a woman's hair
And woman's hands, and now was like a vine
That wrapped him round with leaves and sudden flowers,
And now was like a huge white thistledown
Floating; and with this changing shape he fought
Furious and exhausted, till at length
I saw him fall upon it in the sand
And strangle it. Its tentacles of leaves
Fell weakly downward from his back, its flowers
Turned black. And then, as he had whirled at first,
So whirled he now again, and with his feet
Drew out the sand, and made a pit, and flung
The scorpion-woman-vine therein, and heaped
The sand above.

                    And then I heard him sing
And saw him dance; and all that swollen plain

Where no herb grew, became a paradise
Of flowers, and smoking grass, and blowing trees
That shook out birds and song of birds. And he
In power and beauty shining like a demon
Danced there, until that cloud that was a bird
Let fall its wings and darkened him, and hid
The shining fields. But still for long I heard
His voice, and bird-song bells about him chiming,
And knew him dancing there above that grave.

III

Said he: Thus draw your secret sorrow forth,
Whether it wear a woman's face or not;
Walk there at dusk beside that grove of trees,
And sing, and she will come. For while she haunts
Your shameful wood with all its webs and wounds
And darkly broods and works her mischief there,
No peace you'll have, but snares, and poisonous flowers
And trees in lamentation. Call her out
As memory cries the white ghost from the tomb.
Play the sharp lyric flute, for that she loves,
With topaz phrases for her vanity.

And I in answer: She is dear to me,
Dearer that in my mind she makes a dark
Of woods and rocks and thorns and venomous flowers.
What matter that I seldom see her face,
Or have her beauty never? She is there,
It is her voice I hear in cries of trees.
This may be misery, but it is blest.

Then he: And when you have her, strongly take
Her protean fiery body and lithe arms
And wailing mouth and growing vines of hair
And leaves that turn to hands, and bear her forth
Into that landscape that is rightly yours
And dig a grave for her, and thrust her in
All writhing, and so cover her with earth.
Then will the two, as should be, fuse in one.

43

The landscape, that was dead, will straightway shine
And sing and flower about you, trees will grow
Where desert was, water will flash from dust,
And rocks grow out in leaves. And you, this grief
Torn from your heart and planted in your world,
Will know yourself at peace.

                But will it be,—
I asked,—as bright a joy to see that landscape
Put on diffused her wonder, sing her name,
Burn with the vital secret of her body
There locked in earth like fire, as now to have
Her single beauty fugitive in my mind?
If she is lost, will flowering rocks give peace?

And he in answer: So you have the landscape
With all her nerves and voices . . . She is yours.

Exile

These hills are sandy. Trees are dwarfed here. Crows
Caw dismally in skies of an arid brilliance,
Complain in dusty pine-trees. Yellow daybreak
Lights on the long brown slopes a frost-like dew,
Dew as heavy as rain; the rabbit tracks
Show sharply in it, as they might in snow.
But it's soon gone in the sun—what good does it do?
The houses, on the slope, or among brown trees,
Are grey and shrivelled. And the men who live here
Are small and withered, spider-like, with large eyes.

Bring water with you if you come to live here—
Cold tinkling cisterns, or else wells so deep
That one looks down to Ganges or Himalayas.
Yes, and bring mountains with you, white, moon-bearing,

Mountains of ice. You will have need of these
Profundities and peaks of wet and cold.

Bring also, in a cage of wire or osier,
Birds of a golden colour, who will sing
Of leaves that do not wither, watery fruits
That heavily hang on long melodious boughs
In the blue-silver forests of deep valleys.

I have now been here—how many years? Years unnumbered.
My hands grow clawlike. My eyes are large and starved.
I brought no bird with me, I have no cistern
Where I might find the moon, or river, or snow.
Some day, for lack of these, I'll spin a web
Between two dusty pine-tree tops, and hang there
Face downward, like a spider, blown as lightly
As ghost of leaf. Crows will caw about me.
Morning and evening I shall drink the dew.

Samadhi

Take then the music; plunge in the thickest of it,—
Thickest, darkest, richest; call it a forest,
A million boles of trees, with leaves, leaves,
Golden and green, flashing like scales in the sun,
Tossed and torn in the tempest, whirling and streaming,
With the terrible sound, beneath, of boughs that crack.
. . . Again, a hush comes; and the wind's a whisper.
One leaf goes pirouetting. You stand in the dusk
In the misty shaft of light the sun flings faintly
Through planes of green; and suddenly, out of the darkest
And deepest and furthest of the forest ,wavers
That golden horn, *cor anglais*, husky-timbred,
Sending through all this gloom of trees and silence
Its faint half-mute nostalgia . . . How the soul

Flies from the dungeon of you to the very portals
To meet that sound! There, there, is the secret
Singing out of the darkness,—shining, too,
For all we know, if we could only see!
But if we steal by footpaths, warily,—
Snap not a twig, nor crush a single leaf;
Or if, in a kind of panic, like wild beasts,
We rend our violent way through vines and briars,
Crash through a coppice, tear our flesh, come bleeding
To a still pool, encircled, brooded over
By ancient trees—all's one! We reach but silence,
We find no horn, no hornsman . . . There the beeches
Out of the lower dark of ferns and mosses
Lift, far above, their tremulous tops to the light.
Only an echo hear we of that horn,
Cor anglais, golden, husky-timbred, crying
Half-mute nostalgia from the dark of things . . .
Then, as we stand bewildered in that wood,
With leaves above us in sibilant confusion,
And the ancient ghosts of leaves about our feet—
Listen!—the horn once more, but farther now,
Sings in the evening for a wing-beat space;
Makes the leaves murmur, as it makes the blood
Burn in the heart and all its radiant veins;
And we turn inward, to seek it once again.

Or, it's a morning in the blue portal of summer.
White shoals of little clouds, like heavenly fish,
Swim softly off the sun, who rains his light
On the vast hurrying earth. The giant poplar
Sings in the light with a thousand sensitive leaves,
Root-tip to leaf-tip he is all delight:
And, at the golden core of all that joy,
One sinister grackle with a thievish eye
Scrapes a harsh cynic comment. How he laughs,
Flaunting amid that green his coffin-colour!
We, in the garden a million miles below him,
At paltry tasks of pruning, spading, watching
Black-stripèd bees crawl into foxglove bells
Half-filled with dew—look! we are lightly startled
By sense or sound; are moved; lose touch with earth;

And, in the twinkling of the grackle's eye,
Swing in the infinite on a spider's cable.
What is our world? It is a poplar tree
Immense and solitary, with leaves a thousand,
Or million, countless, flashing in a light
For them alone intended. He is great,
His trunk is solid, and his roots deceive us.
We shade our eyes with hands and upward look
To see if all those leaves indeed be leaves,
So rich they are in a choiring down of joy,
Or stars. And as we stand so, small and dumb,
We hear again that harsh derisive comment,
The grackle's laughter; and again we see
His thievish eye, aware amid green boughs.
Touch earth again: take up your shovel: dig
In the wormy ground. That tree magnificent
Sways like a giant dancer in a garment
Whose gold and green are naught but tricks of light.
And at the heart of all that drunken beauty
Is a small lively cynic bird who laughs.

Who sees the vision coming? Who can tell
What moment out of time will be the seed
To root itself, as swift as lightning roots
Into a cloud, and grow, swifter than thought,
And flower gigantic in the infinite?
Walk softly through your forest, and be ready
To hear the horn of horns. Or in your garden
Stoop, but upon your back be ever conscious
Of sunlight, and a shadow that may grow.

King Borborigmi

You say you heard King Borborigmi laugh?
Say how it was. Some heavenly body moved him?
The moon laughed first? Dark earth put up a finger
Of honeysuckle, through his moonlit window,
And tickled him?

                    King Borborigmi laughed
Alone, walking alone in an empty room,
Thinking, and yet not thinking, seeing, yet blind.
One hand was on his chin, feeling the beard
That razors could not stay; the other groped;
For it was dark, and in the dark were chairs;
Midnight, or almost midnight; Aldebaran
Hanging among the dews.

                    King Borborigmi
Laughed once or twice at nothing, just as midnight
Released a flock of bells?

                    Not this alone;
Not bells in flight toward Aldebaran;
Nor the immitigable beard; nor dews
Heavily pattering on the pent-house roof;
Nor chairs in shadow which his foot disturbed.
Yet it was all of these, and more: the air
Twirling the curtain where a red moth hung:
The one bell flying later than the others
Into the starstrung silence: the garden breaking
To let a thousand seedlings have their way:
An eye-tooth aching, and the pendulum
That heavily ticked upon the leftward swing.

—These trifles woke the laughter of a king?

—Much less than these, and more! He softly stepped
Among the webby world, and felt it shudder.
Under the earth—a strand or two of web—
He saw his father's bones, fallen apart,
The jawbone sunken and the skull caved in.
Among his mother's bones a cactus rooted,
And two moles crept, and ants held carnival.
Above the obscene tomb an aloe blossomed;
Dew glistened on the marble. This he saw,
And at the selfsame moment heard the cook
Wind the alarm-clock in her bedroom, yawn,
And creak the bed. And it was then, surprised,
He touched a chair, and laughed, and twitched the curtain,—
And the moth flew out.

      —Alas, poor Borborigmi,
That it should be so little, and so sorry
A thing to make him laugh!

       —Young Borborigmi,
Saw more than this. The infinite octopus
With eyes of chaos and long arms of stars,
And belly of void and darkness, became clear
About him, and he saw himself embraced
And swept along a vein, with chairs and teeth,
Houses and bones and gardens, cooks and clocks;
The midnight bell, a snoring cook, and he,
Mingled and flowed like atoms.

        —It was this
That made him laugh—to see himself as one
Corpuscle in the infinite octopus? . . .
And was this all, old fool, old turner of leaves? . . .

—Alone, thinking alone in an empty room
Where moonlight and the mouse were met together,
And pulse and clock together ticked, and dew
Made contrapuntal patter, Borborigmi
Fathomed in his own viscera the world,
Went downward, sounding like a diver, holding
His peakèd nose; and when he came up, laughed.
These things and others saw. But last of all,
Ultimate or penultimate, he saw
The one thing that undid him!

      —What was this?
The one grotesquer thing among grotesques?
Carrion, offal, or the toothbrush ready
For carnal fangs? Cancer, that grasps the heart,
Or fungus, whitely swelling in the brain?
Some gargoyle of the thought?

      King Borborigmi,
Twitching the curtain as the last bell flew
Melodious to Aldebaran, beheld
The moth fly also. Downward dropped it softly
Among dropped petals, white. And there one rose

Was open in the moonlight! Dew was on it;
The bat, with ragged wing, cavorting, sidling,
Snapped there a sleeping bee—

              And crunched the moth? . . .

—It was the rose in moonlight, crimson, yet
Blanched by the moon; the bee asleep; the bat
And fallen moth—but most the guileless rose.
Guileless! . . . King Borborigmi struck his foot
Against a chair, and saw the guileless rose
Joining himself (King Bubblegut), and all
Those others—the immitigable beard;
Razors and teeth; his mother's bones; the tomb:
The yawning cook; the clock; the dew; the bells
Bursting upward like bubbles—; all so swept
Along one vein of the infinite octopus
With eyes of chaos and long arms of stars
And belly of void and darkness. It was then
He laughed; as he would never laugh again.
For he saw everything; and, in the centre
Of corrupt change, one guileless rose; and laughed
For puzzlement and sorrow.

              Ah, poor man,
Poor Borborigmi, young, to be so wise!

—Wise? No. For what he laughed at was just this:
That to see all, to know all, is to rot.
So went to bed; and slept; is sleeping still,
If none has waked him.

            —Dead? King Borborigmi
Is dead? Died laughing? Sleeps a dreamless sleep
Till cook's alarm clock wakes him?

            —Sleeps like Hamlet,
King of infinite space in a walnut shell—
But has bad dreams; I fear he has bad dreams.

And in the Hanging Gardens

And in the hanging gardens there is rain
From midnight until one, striking the leaves
And bells of flowers, and stroking boles of planes,
And drawing slow arpeggios over pools,
And stretching strings of sound from eaves to ferns.
The princess reads. The knave of diamonds sleeps.
The king is drunk, and flings a golden goblet
Down from the turret window (curtained with rain)
Into the lilacs.

                    And at one o'clock
The vulcan under the garden wakes and beats
The gong upon his anvil. Then the rain
Ceases, but gently ceases, dripping still,
And sound of falling water fills the dark
As leaves grow bold and upright, and as eaves
Part with water. The princess turns the page
Beside the candle, and between two braids
Of golden hair. And reads: 'From there I went
Northward a journey of four days, and came
To a wild village in the hills, where none
Was living save the vulture and the rat,
And one old man, who laughed, but could not speak.
The roofs were fallen in; the well grown over
With weed; and it was there my father died.
Then eight days further, bearing slightly west,
The cold wind blowing sand against our faces,
The food tasting of sand. And as we stood
By the dry rock that marks the highest point
My brother said: "Not too late is it yet
To turn, remembering home." And we were silent
Thinking of home.' The princess shuts her eyes
And feels the tears forming beneath her eyelids

And opens them, and tears fall on the page.
The knave of diamonds in the darkened room
Throws off his covers, sleeps, and snores again.
The king goes slowly down the turret stairs
To find the goblet.

And at two o'clock
The vulcan in his smithy underground
Under the hanging gardens, where the drip
Of rain among the clematis and ivy
Still falls from sipping flower to purple flower,
Smites twice his anvil, and the murmur comes
Among the roots and vines. The princess reads:
'As I am sick, and cannot write you more,
Nor have not long to live, I give this letter
To him, my brother, who will bear it south
And tell you how I died. Ask how it was,
There in the northern desert, where the grass
Was withered, and the horses, all but one,
Perished' . . . The princess drops her golden head
Upon the page between her two white arms
And golden braids. The knave of diamonds wakes
And at his window in the darkened room
Watches the lilacs tossing, where the king
Seeks for the goblet.

And at three o'clock
The moon inflames the lilac heads, and thrice
The vulcan, in his root-bound smithy, clangs
His anvil; and the sounds creep softly up
Among the vines and walls. The moon is round,
Round as a shield above the turret top.
The princess blows her candle out, and weeps
In the pale room, where scent of lilac comes,
Weeping, with hands across her eyelids, thinking
Of withered grass, withered by sandy wind.
The knave of diamonds, in his darkened room,
Holds in his hands a key, and softly steps
Along the corridor, and slides the key
Into the door that guards her. Meanwhile, slowly,
The king, with raindrops on his beard and hands,

And dripping sleeves, climbs up the turret stairs,
Holding the goblet upright in one hand;
And pauses on the midmost step, to taste
One drop of wine, wherewith wild rain has mixed.

The Wedding

At noon, Tithonus, withered by his singing,
Climbing the oatstalk with his hairy legs,
Met grey Arachne, poisoned and shrunk down
By her own beauty; pride had shrivelled both.
In the white web—where seven flies hung wrapped—
She heard his footstep; hurried to him; bound him;
Enshrouded him in silk; then poisoned him.
Twice shrieked Tithonus, feebly; then was still.
Arachne loved him. Did he love Arachne?
She watched him with red eyes, venomous sparks,
And the furred claws outspread . . . 'O sweet Tithonus!
Darling! Be kind, and sing that song again!
Shake the bright web again with that deep fiddling!
Are you much poisoned? sleeping? do you dream?
Darling Tithonus!'

                    And Tithonus, weakly
Moving one hairy shin against the other
Within the silken sack, contrived to fiddle
A little tune, half-hearted: 'Shrewd Arachne!
Whom pride in beauty withered to this shape
As pride in singing shrivelled me to mine—
Unwrap me, let me go—and let me limp,
With what poor strength your venom leaves me, down
This oatstalk, and away.'

                    Arachne, angry,
Stung him again, twirling him with rough paws,
The red eyes keen. 'What! You would dare to leave me?

Unkind Tithonus! Sooner I'll kill and eat you
Than let you go. But sing that tune again—
So plaintive was it!'

          And Tithonus faintly
Moved the poor fiddles, which were growing cold,
And sang: 'Arachne, goddess envied of gods,
Beauty's eclipse eclipsed by angry beauty,
Have pity, do not ask the withered heart
To sing too long for you! My strength goes out,
Too late we meet for love. O be content
With friendship, which the noon sun once may kindle
To give one flash of passion, like a dewdrop,
Before it goes! . . . Be reasonable,—Arachne!'

Arachne heard the song grow weaker, dwindle
To first a rustle, and then half a rustle,
And last a tick, so small no ear could hear it
Save hers, a spider's ear. And her small heart,
(Rusted away, like his, to a pinch of dust,)
Gleamed once, like his, and died. She clasped him tightly
And sunk her fangs in him. Titnonus dead,
She slept awhile, her last sensation gone;
Woke from the nap, forgetting him; and ate him.

The Road

Three then came forward out of darkness, one
An old man bearded, his old eyes red with weeping,
A peasant, with hard hands. 'Come now,' he said,
'And see the road, for which our people die.
Twelve miles of road we've made, a little only,
Westward winding. Of human blood and stone
We build; and in a thousand years will come
Beyond the hills to sea.'

I went with them,
Taking a lantern, which upon their faces
Showed years and grief; and in a time we came
To the wild road which wound among wild hills
Westward; and so along this road we stooped,
Silent, thinking of all the dead men, there
Compounded with sad clay. Slowly we moved:
For they were old and weak, had given all
Their life, to build this twelve poor miles of road,
Muddy, under the rain. And in my hand
Turning the lantern, here or there, I saw
Deep holes of water where the raindrop splashed,
And rainfilled footprints in the grass, and heaps
Of broken stone, and rusted spades and picks,
And helves of axes. And the old man spoke,
Holding my wrist: 'Three hundred years it took
To build these miles of road: three hundred years;
And human lives unnumbered. But the day
Will come when it is done.' Then spoke another,
One not so old, but old, whose face was wrinkled:
'And when it comes, our people will all sing
For joy, passing from east to west, or west
To east, returning, with the light behind them;
All meeting in the road and singing there.'
And the third said: 'The road will be their life;
A heritage of blood. Grief will be in it,
And beauty out of grief. And I can see
How all the women's faces will be bright.
In that time, laughing, they will remember us.
Blow out your lantern now, for day is coming.'
My lantern blown out, in a little while
We climbed in long light up a hill, where climbed
The dwindling road, and ended in a field.
Peasants were working in the field, bowed down
With unrewarded work, and grief, and years
Of pain. And as we passed them, one man fell
Into a furrow that was bright with water
And gave a cry that was half cry half song—
'The road . . . the road . . . the road . . .' And all then fell
Upon their knees and sang.

We four passed on
Over the hill, to westward. Then I felt
How tears ran down my face, tears without number;
And knew that all my life henceforth was weeping,
Weeping, thinking of human grief, and human
Endeavour fruitless in a world of pain.
And when I held my hands up they were old;
I knew my face would not be young again.

Dead Leaf in May

One skeleton-leaf, white-ribbed, a last year's leaf,
Skipped in a paltry gust, whizzed from the dust,
Leapt the small dusty puddle; and sailing then
Merrily in the sunlight, lodged itself
Between two blossoms in a hawthorn tree.
That was the moment: and the world was changed.
With that insane gay skeleton of a leaf
A world of dead worlds flew to hawthorn trees,
Lodged in the green forks, rattled, rattled their ribs
(As loudly as a dead leaf's ribs can rattle)
Blithely, among bees and blossoms. I cursed,
I shook my stick, dislodged it. To what end?
Its ribs, and all the ribs of all dead worlds,
Would house them now forever as death should:
Cheek by jowl with May.

That was the moment: and my brain flew open
Like a ripe bursting pod. The seed sprang out,
And I was withered, and had given all.
Ripeness at top means rottenness beneath:
The brain divulging seed, the heart is empty:
The little blood goes through it like quicksilver:
The hand is leather, and the world is lost.

Human, who trudge the road from Here to There:
Lock the dry oak-leaf's flimsy skeleton
In auricle or ventricle; sail it
Like a gay ship down red Aorta's flood.
Be the paired blossoms with dead ribs between.
Thirst in the There, that you may drink the Here.

Sea Holly

Begotten by the meeting of rock with rock,
The mating of rock and rock, rocks gnashing together;
Created so, and yet forgetful, walks
The seaward path, puts up her left hand, shades
Blue eyes, the eyes of rock, to see better
In slanting light the ancient sheep (which kneels
Biting the grass) the while her other hand,
Hooking the wicker handle, turns the basket
Of eggs. The sea is high to-day. The eggs
Are cheaper. The sea is blown from the southwest,
Confused, taking up sand and mud in waves,
The waves break, sluggish, in brown foam, the wind
Disperses (on the sheep and hawthorn) spray,—
And on her cheeks, the cheeks engendered of rock,
And eyes, the colour of rock. The left hand
Falls from the eyes, and undecided slides
Over the left breast on which muslin lightly
Rests, touching the nipple, and then down
The hollow side, virgin as rock, and bitterly
Caresses the blue hip.

It was for this,
This obtuse taking of the seaward path,
This stupid hearing of larks, this hooking
Of wicker, this absent observation of sheep
Kneeling in harsh sea-grass, the cool hand shading

The spray-stung eyes—it was for this the rock
Smote itself. The sea is higher to-day,
And eggs are cheaper. The eyes of rock take in
The seaward path that winds toward the sea,
The thistle-prodder, old woman under a bonnet,
Forking the thistles, her back against the sea,
Pausing, with hard hands on the handle, peering
With rock eyes from her bonnet.

              It was for this,
This rock-lipped facing of brown waves, half sand
And half water, this tentative hand that slides
Over the breast of rock, and into the hollow
Soft side of muslin rock, and then fiercely
Almost as rock against the hip of rock—
It was for this in midnight the rocks met,
And dithered together, cracking and smoking.

              It was for this
Barren beauty, barrenness of rock that aches
On the seaward path, seeing the fruitful sea,
Hearing the lark of rock that sings, smelling
The rock-flower of hawthorn, sweetness of rock—
It was for this, stone pain in the stony heart,
The rock loved and laboured; and all is lost.

The Room

Through that window—all else being extinct
Except itself and me—I saw the struggle
Of darkness against darkness. Within the room
It turned and turned, dived downward. Then I saw
How order might—if chaos wished—become:
And saw the darkness crush upon itself,
Contracting powerfully; it was as if
It killed itself: slowly: and with much pain.

Pain. The scene was pain, and nothing but pain.
What else, when chaos draws all forces inward
To shape a single leaf? . . .

For the leaf came,
Alone and shining in the empty room;
After a while the twig shot downward from it;
And from the twig a bough; and then the trunk,
Massive and coarse; and last the one black root.
The black root cracked the walls. Boughs burst the window:
The great tree took possession.

Tree of trees!
Remember (when time comes) how chaos died
To shape the shining leaf. Then turn, have courage,
Wrap arms and roots together, be convulsed
With grief, and bring back chaos out of shape.
I will be watching then as I watch now.
I will praise darkness now, but then the leaf.

Sound of Breaking

Why do you cry out, why do I like to hear you
Cry out, here in the dewless evening, sitting
Close, close together, so close that the heart stops beating
And the brain its thought? Wordless, worthless mortals
Stumbling, exhausted, in this wilderness
Of our conjoint destruction! Hear the grass
Raging about us! Hear the worms applaud!
Hear how the ripples make a sound of chaos!
Hear now, in these and the other sounds of evening,
The first brute step of God!

About your elbow,
Making a ring of thumb and finger, I
Slide the walled blood against the less-walled blood,

Move down your arm, surmount the wrist-bone, shut
Your long slim hand in mine. Each finger-tip
Is then saluted by a finger-tip;
The hands meet back to back, then face to face;
Then lock together. And we, with eyes averted,
Smile at the evening sky of alabaster,
See nothing, lose our souls in the maelstrom, turning
Downward in rapid circles.

            Bitter woman,
Bitter of heart and brain and blood, bitter as I
Who drink your bitterness—can this be beauty?
Do you cry out because the beauty is cruel?
Terror, because we downward sweep so swiftly?
Terror of darkness?

           It is a sound of breaking,
The world is breaking, the world is a sound of breaking,
Many-harmonied, diverse, profound,
A shattering beauty. See, how together we break,
Hear what a crashing of disordered chords and discords
Fills the world with falling, when we thus lean
Our two mad bodies together!

           It is a sound
Of everlasting grief, the sound of weeping,
The sound of disaster and misery, the sound
Of passionate heartbreak at the centre of the world.

Electra

       I

The little princess, on her eleventh birthday,
Trapped a blue butterfly in a net of gauze,
Where it was sunning on a speckled stone.
The blue wings fluttered in the silkworm net.

'What voice, Blue Butterfly,' (the Princess cried)
'Is voice of butterfly? . . . You scream in fury
Close to my ear; yet hear I not a sound.'
She caught it down against the stone, and pressed
A royal finger on each round blue wing;
And as one tears apart a folded leaf
By pushing right and left, so tore she, smiling,
The azure fly . . . Her eyes were bright and blue,
Her teeth were sharp; the sunlight streaked her hair
With twining gold along two braids. She frowned
As might a chemist at a test-tube-drop
(Bright, poisonous and pendent) when she saw
Cerulean dust upon each finger tip.
This, being rubbed against a tulip-mouth,
(A glutted bee dislodged) she sat demurely:
Opened her book, on which leaf-shadows winked;
And blew a dart toward a scarlet bird
In bright green tropics of the Amazon.

II

Dressing the naked doll of redded wax,
(The white cheeks rouged), she feather-stitched a square
Of scarlet silk with golden staggering stitches;
Chain-lightninged all its edges. After this,
A square of azure silk, a square of purple,
Superimposed; and then a tinfoil crown,
Massive, of divers colours; this, compounded
(Relics of Beaune, of Jerez, and Oporto)
Blazed the wax brow. A bed of cottonwool
Was smoothed; and thrice-anointed Ferdinand
(First pressed against her thigh for nourishment)
Was covered with a soiled green handkerchief
And closed his eyes: exchanging glass for wax.

This was the seventh year. Between the eighth
And ninth, the form of nourishment was changed.
The doll was clasped between her knees. She held
A knife in one hand, while the other lifted
A paper bird. The neck of this was severed.
And Ferdinand had passed from milk to blood.

'Your soul' (so said her father in the spring
That brought her sixteenth year) 'turns smaller, as
Your body waxes to ripe beauty. Dwarfs
(As you have seen in circuses, or tumbling
Through scarlet-papered hoops, at vaudeville)
Bear on the brow, though mouth and eyes be fair,
A drawn and arid look, of suffering.
Dwarfed, and as blue and arid, peers the soul
Like a starved nymph from your bright eyes. Your mouth
Though beautiful, and, yes, desirable,—
(Even to me, who like a wizard shaped it),—
Is much too red; too cruelly downward curved,
It hides a tooth too sharp. You will do murder—
Laughing and weeping; hear the song of blood;
The gnome in you will laugh; the nymph will weep.'

She locked strong hands around his neck and kissed him.
Lifting a naked knee to press him subtly
She hurt him consciously; kissed till he laughed;
Unlocked her hands, then, sobered; moved away;
Shook down the golden skirt; whistled a tune;
And read the morning paper, coiled like a cat.

IV

'Under this water-lily knee' (she said)
'Blood intricately flows, corpuscle creeps,
The white like sliced cucumber, and the red
Like poker-chip! Along dark mains they flow
As wafts the sponging heart. The water-lily,
Subtle in seeming, bland to lover's hand
Upthrust exploring, is in essence gross,
Multiple and corrupt. Thus, in the moonlight'
(She hooked a curtain and disclosed the moon)
'How cold and lucent! And this naked breast,
Whereon a blue vein writes Diana's secret,
How simple! How seductive of the palm
That flatters with the finest tact of flesh!

Not silver is this flank, nor ivory,
Gold it is not, not copper, but distilled
Of lust in moonlight, and my own hand strays
To touch it in this moonlight, whence it came.'
Naked in moonlight, like a doll of wax,
On the stone floor nocturnal, she stood still
But moved her hands. The cruel mouth was curved,
Smiling a little; and her eyes were fixed,
In wonder, on Diana's hieroglyph.
And it was then (her nineteenth autumn come)
She heard at last, so often prophesied,
The singing of the blood. Her beauty broke
To sound beneath her hands, which moved from breast
To knee and back again, and bruised the flank
That was not gold or copper, but became
A throbbing sound beneath palpating palms.
Thus stood awhile; then sighed; then dropped her hands
And wept, as he (who loved her) had foretold.

v

It was the twentieth birthday, or the moon,
Which flung a careless net upon the house
Trapping the stone (as she had trapped the fly);
These, or the emptied heart of night, which filled
The house with weeping. In the room they lay
Weeping together. 'Like a harp it is'
(She said) 'which but to sound, but once to sound,
Snaps every string. Better to die, than be
Conjointly now, henceforth, a broken thing
Where sound of life was once.' She pressed his hand
Against her side, where once the doll was pressed,
Prince Ferdinand; but she was hungry still.
So then she held him hard between her knees
And heard the song of blood, outrageously,
And cried, 'Shut eyes and kiss me!' 'O, Arachne!
What web is this you weave, dear poison-mouth?'
'The web, alas, is cut as soon as woven,'
She answered. And the word she spoke was true.

The moonlight and the house then sang together,
Yet not the house, but something in the house,
As if together they once more distilled
(Of blood and moonlight) ivory or gold,
Copper or silver; or, if not quite these
Something of which the moon contrived the surface
While blood beneath supplied the essence gross.
Useless! for it was spilled as soon as brimmed.
Prince Ferdinand was dead, Arachne dead,
The blood unmoving, and the moonlight vain.

The Pomecitron Tree

Here the skeleton leaf, between
Eglantine and celandine,
Harries an hour (that seems an age)
The snail's deliberate pilgrimage.
And in that same stupendous hour,
While royally unfolds the flower
Magniloquent in the sunlight, She
Dreams by the pomecitron tree.

Not lust alone is in her mind,
Nor the sad shapes of humankind.
What ant is this, with horns, who comes
Exploring huge geraniums?
Up the green-jointed column stalks,
And into halls of scarlet walks;
Boldly intrudes, partakes, then goes
—Alas!—to eat her favorite rose.

Not lust alone; yet this was lust,
And lust was that deliberate gust

That warmly roused the leaves, caressed
The lawn, and on her open breast
Blew, from the pomecitron tree,
One ravished petal, and a bee . . .
Into her bosom flew, from this,
The fiery-wingèd wounding kiss.

Into her bosom. Deeper then,
It startles to that world of men,
Who, in the kingdom of her mind,
Awake, arise, begin to wind
Along the subterranean road
That leads from their abhorred abode . . .
They move and murmur, while the ant
Climbs an enormous rhubarb plant.

And then it is her voice that cries,
While still beneath the tree she lies:
Maker of gardens, let me be
Turned to a pomecitron tree!
Within his veins no longings rise;
He turns no concupiscent eyes;
Nor hears, in the infernal mind,
The lustful army wake and wind.

He, though his roots are in the grave,
Is placid and unconscious, save
Of burning light, or rain, that slides
On dripping leaves and down his sides.
In his cool thought the sparrow nests;
A leaf, among more leaves she rests;
Or, if she sings, her watery voice
Is joined with countless that rejoice.

What bliss is his! what deep delight!
To face, with his own dark, the night!
With his own sunrise meet the sun!
Or whistle with the wind, and run!
Why, Lord, was it ordained that I
Must turn an inward-roving eye?

Why must I know, unlike this tree,
What lusts and murders nourish me?

To him, no doubt, most innocent
Seems, in this sunlight, my intent:
No primrose ever lightlier breathed
Than my tall body, flower-enwreathed.
Soft as lilies the sunlight rests
Upon my pollen-powdered breasts.
My two hands, of their own sweet will,
Can stir like leaves, or stand as still.

What stems can match this throat of gold
And ivory? What stalks uphold
So lightly, in this garden, such
Delirious flowers to taste and touch?
What pistilled mouth can rival here
My mouth, what leaves outvie my hair
In mindless beauty? . . . Yet, behind
This mindless beauty lurks a mind.

Ah, while the rhubarb leaf is spread
Broad as a salver by my head:
And the green aphis pastures on
This tall green tower of Solomon:
The mind, within my flower's bell,
Conceals its black concentric hell.
There at this minute swarms the host,
And lewd ghost speaks with furious ghost.

There the sad shapes of humankind
Through brown defiles in sorrow wind;
And, if they speak, their arid speech
Is of that land they cannot reach.
There the defeated warrior lies,
And westward turns defrauded eyes.
Deformed and monstrous are those men:
They climb, and do not turn again.

It is to me each lifts his face!
It is to me, with footsore pace,

Summoned once more, they creep and come,
Pointing toward me as to home.
What love is in their eyes! Alas,
That love so soon to lust should pass!
The hands they lift are stumps; they stir
The rank leaves where their faces were.

Maker of gardens, let me be
Turned to a pomecitron tree;
Or let me be this rhubarb plant,
Whose lavish love is ignorant;
Or let me be this daffodil,
Which lusts and murders, yet is still
All-in-itself, a golden All
Concentred in one burning ball!

. . . She sighs; and it is in her thought
That grief so desperate may be fraught
With tears; and tears were sweet, displayed
Here, in the pomecitron shade;
And grief is pleasant, when beguiled
By mindless garden, or a child;
But the few tears are thought, not shed;
She claps her hands, and laughs, instead.

Changing Mind

1

The room filled with the sound of voices,
The voices weaving like vines or voices of viols,
And the voices mixed, filling the warm room
From wall to vibrant wall. It was then I saw
The talk itself, the fourfold torrent of talk
(Below the candles and above the fire)
Moving like golden water!

'Come under!' he said,
'Come down under the talk! Stoop your shoulders
And enter the darkness!'

          Who could this be
Who spoke to me in secret, while those others
Wove with their spider-mouths the moving water?
It was not the small man, not the tall man,
And not the woman whose long hair of burnt gold
Fell on the talk and was woven into it;
Nor was it that other woman, who blew smoke
Over the golden hair and golden water.

          'Come under!' he said;
And as he spoke I saw him! His white face
Came up laughing, with bright hair! He showed
(Turning upon his axis, a strong swimmer
Making himself a ball) how he could scoop
A hollow in bright air, turning within it;
His white arms, curving like a swimmer's, shaped
The dark sphere out of brightness. There he curled,
In that cold chrysalis, secret under the talk,
Carved in the light.

          'You! Narcissus!' I said!
And softly, under the four-voiced dialogue,
In the bright ether, in the golden river
Of cabbalistic sound, I plunged, I found
The silver rind of peace, the hollow round
Carved out of nothing; curled there like a god.

The blue-eyed woman, leaning above the water,
Shook her scarab ear-rings, while her voice
Entered the stream. 'Nevertheless'—she said—
Leaning toward the golden foam her head—
'Nevertheless I am not dead;
Let him forget me at his peril!'—this she said,
Smiling, and showing the three rings on her finger,
The fourth of her left hand. Her arm was naked,
The low green bodice showed her bosom rising,

Rising more quickly, as with agitation.
'I can entice him still, my eye is quick
As a lizard's eye, my tongue is quick—'

       '—as quick
As an aspic's!'—this the tall man rang, and laughed.
The small man also laughed, and the bright stream
Rose deeper; and I felt myself submerged,
Submerged deliciously.

       The small man whistled:
After the four dull boulders of their laugh
Had sunk beside me, sending up four spouts
Of golden water. The long whistle
Ran like a nerve. It was blue, and reached
At the near end a gong, and at the far
A copper spring. This all four pressed at once,
And the long screaming nerve wound through the water,
While they above it leaned. Ah, did they see
How the blue nerve was grounded twice in me?
'Laugh if you like,' she said, whose golden hair
Fell round me fine as water-sifted sunlight,
'Whistle derision from Rome to Jericho;
Sell him to Doctor Wundt the psycho-analyst
Whose sex-ray eyes will separate him out
Into a handful of blank syllables,—
Like a grammarian, whose beak can parse
A sentence till its gaudy words mean nothing;
Yet if I smile above him, ah, you'll see!
Each idiot syllable of what was once
The multitudinous meaning of that brain
Will beat devotion and speak its love again!'

(Alas, it is true I am dispersed thus,
Dissected out on the glass-topped table,
The tweezers picking up syllables and putting them down,
Particles so small they have no colour;
I am dispersed, and yet I know
That sovereign eye, if once it glare its love,
Will reassemble me.)

The other woman,
Blowing her smoke above the outspread hair
And woven water and hair, and the dying nerve
Of sibilation, spoke at last, and while she spoke
I saw the four walls leaning inward above the stream,
And her with the rings upon her fingers, leaning,
And the two men smiling above me.
Venus too was there, and the evening star,
And the inverted trees, and the terror-coloured sky.
Sky, trees, walls, gods, birds.

'Let him forget you at his peril, this you say?
O Alba, what a bloody jest is here!
If he remember you, the peril is yours.
You, then, are only you? this gold-ring-fingered,
Green-bodiced leman? No, no, be not deceived!
You are not only you, this one great golden
Goddess above the stream with sovereign eye!
You are not only the sea-cold marble, interfused
With sanguine warmth, yet pure as the sea-coral!
You are not only the one white god of forked
Flesh, bewildering ever, never sating!
How could this be?'

                She blew a round blue cloud
Of smoke across the golden moving water,
(Whereunder in my hollow I sat sleeping)
And smiled.

       'How could this be? You are but one
Of all our host; and us too he has seen.
Us he remembers when he remembers you:
The livid; the sore; the old; the worn; the wounded:
Hating the smell of us, you too he'll hate.
Ah, Alba, what a cruel jest is here!
For if you wake him, with that sovereign eye,
Teasing his flesh with the three-gold-ringed finger
Until, assembled, he again swims up:
Will it not be to me—to me also—he comes?
Me, the dead cormorant whom he so loathed
And buried by the sea?'

                        She leaned, and then
I saw her weeping. Intolerable pity
Broke in my heart when thus I saw her weeping.
Her in blue muslin, tall and meagre, her
The starved blue cormorant whom I betrayed.

Then Doctor Wundt, the tall man, walked beside
The sparkling stream. His face was like a star.
Between the leaves, inexorable, he shone,
While the brown thrush, sequestered, hushed the wood
With meditative song. Anon the youths
Came from the wood and laughed with Socrates:
They saw him drink the hemlock, heard him say
Alpha and Omega. Thence up the hill
To Golgotha they jeered, and with them took
The sponge, the spear, the flask of vinegar,
And that poor king, whose madness, on a Friday,
Burned to a beauty like the evening star.
Hegel, too, came shoreward in that evening,
Leaning above me, leaning above the stream,
Whose motion (so he sighed at length) was only
Manifestation of the dialectic.
And others, too; some singly, some in groups,
Talking a little, or silent. There at last
My father also came. The dead leaf's step
Was his, rapid and light; and his young face
Shone like the evening star, inexorable.

And he and Doctor Wundt together spoke,
Flinging one image on the moving water,
With one voice spoke, wherewith the bird's voice chimed;
But what it was they said I could not hear.
Only, I heard the bird-voice tinkling 'peace'
Among the lapping leaves, and sound of weeping
Where the tall woman, the blue-muslined, leaned
Above the river; while the sovereign eye
Glared on the water to assemble me.
'Inheritor!'—this word my father said,
And Doctor Wundt said also. The word hung
Smokelike above the stream.

                                          71

2

O Alba! Look! While thus Narcissus sleeps
Under the river, and beside him keeps
Conscious and yet unconscious my bright soul!
Look, how the dawn, the giant swimmer, comes
Over the sky, head downward, swimming slowly,
With powerful bright arms! Out of the east
The blue god looms, and with him come new worlds.
Those bubbles—look—that from his silver heel
Sparkle and burst, and those that from his mouth
Spiral, and those that bead his sides with light,
And those that globe his fingers—those are worlds,
That bursting seem to escape the godlike tether,
And yet do not escape. Is it from me they come—
From me to me? And is that sky myself?

It was the southeast wind, changing softly,
Who thus, eyes downward, swam upon my sky,
Bringing news of the southeast. The weather-vanes—
Golden cocks, ships, and a hundred arrows,—
All creaked at once, changed on a mile of steeples,
All changed at once, as thus the swimmer passed.
And all those bubbles
Whirling about him, voluting sleekly, bursting
With altered shape enlarged, these were the news
Of another country! These were the fields of corn!
These were the salt marshes, steaming in sunlight, where
The herons rise with trailed legs
And the wild horses stamp!
There, in long brightness, breaks the world-long sea!

                              The small man brooded
Darkly above me, darkly glowing,
Mephistopheles, holding in his wide hand
All these shapes. 'It is the kite country,'
He laughed, 'it is the land of kites; and there he walks.'
. . . And as he glowed above me, Chinese lantern
Burning with grinning mouth beneath the leaves,

And the pierced eyes cruel as the eyes of the kite-flyers,
Those others laughed: the tall man first, and then
More musically, melodious derision,
She who had wept, the cormorant, and she
Who threatened, glaring, to assemble me.
Ha, ha, they laughed, descending scale of scorn.
Three towers leaned above me, beating bells,
So that the air was beaten and confused.
Through this (harsh sabbath) mocked the pursuing voice:

'Childe Roland, leaving behind him the dark tower,
Came in the evening to the land of kites.
Peril was past. The skull of the dead horse
His foot broke; and the desert, where wild dogs
Bay up the moon from tall grass, this he crossed
In the long light. And in the kite country—'
(Ha, ha, they laughed, merry descending scale)—
'He saw the diamond kites all rise at once
From the flat land. And on each kite was bound
A weeping woman, the arms outstretched, the feet
Nailed at the foot!'

                        (Alas, how hard it is,
I helpless, bound thus, in my cave, asleep,
Bound in the stinging nerves of sound, these voices!)

'Under the sky of kites he steps, hearing
The sad singing and whimpering of the kites,
Seeing also the blood that drips from hands
Nailed to the Crosspiece, high in air. He climbs
Slowly in twilight to the weeping-cross . . .
Alas, good woman, you no sooner lust
Together concupiscent, your four arms
Enwreathed, your faces fused in one, your eyes
Sightless with foresight of the two-backed beast,
Than with derisive cries and cruel eyes
The kiteflyers come! Your outstretched hands they nail
Against the Crosspiece! Then down the hill they run
Drawing the kitecord with them, so that, weeping,
He hears you, weeping, blown aloft in air!'

Thus the small man, amid derisive laughter!
But it was not of the kites, nor the kite country,
The giant swimmer sang, who brought me news,
News of the southeast! O believe, believe!
Believe, grim four, believe me or I die!
It is from you this vision comes; while I
Dreamed that I swam, and with that swimmer came
Into the southeast of forgotten name.

3

The seven-man orchestra tuned up bubbling and squeaking. Harry Frank, the conductor, stuffed a dirty handkerchief inside his collar, turning goggle eyes to see if his friend Anne was in the audience; and Tom, the drummer, with his prizefighter's mug, was chatting with a couple of skirts in the front row. Lights! Lights! O'Dwyer, his bloodshot eyes, looked round the cherubimed corner of the proscenium arch to see what they were waiting for. What were they waiting for? 'Hearts and Flowers.' Harry rapped his frayed bow on the lamplit tripod, turned his smug Jewish profile from Tom to O'Dwyer, sleekly smiling. He began briskly. The theatre was full. Three thousand faces. Faces in rows like flowers in beds.

And all this, mind you, was myself! myself still asleep under the four-voiced dialogue! the fourfold river of talk! Here the three thousand faces leaned down upon me, stamens and pistils! and here I was the orchestra, a submarine orchestra, a telephone exchange of blue nerves, and a bare stage on which something was about to happen! Here I was Luvic, warbling, her white arms fat at the shoulders, like hams powdered, her green-ringed fingers making in a fold of her dress that pill-rolling motion which is a symptom of paralysis agitans, bugling

> Falling life and fading tree,
> Lines of white in a sullen sea,
> Shadows rising on you and me—

her pale mouth opening and shutting, flexing and reflexing, in perfect time! Here I was Glozo, the card-eater, the ventriloquist, who took goldfish out of his gold-toothed mouth, and Mrs. Glozo, his plump-rumped assistant. Here I was Tozo, the Jap, and his family of little Tozos, all exactly alike in pink fleshings all short-legged and bowlegged, lying on their long backs and twirling purple barrels (gold-star-emblazoned) on their pat-slapping soft feet, tossing the purple barrels from one simian sole to another. Here I was Nozo, the hobo, the awkward inflamed nose with a diamond sparkling on its horn. I was each of these in turn, and then also I was Bozo, the muscular trapeze artist, and all the while I was Harry cocking his left eye over his fiddle, and Tom rubbing sandpaper together (wisha wisha) while Mrs. Bishop put her perfumed hand in his pocket, and three thousand yellow faces perched in rows like birds, and a humming marble foyer with gilt mirrors, and O'Dwyer crowding into the same telephone booth with Mrs. Harry Frank (naughty-naughty) and the electric sign in Bosworth Place—

All this I was, and also the amphitheatre itself,
All this, but also a small room, a forest,
Trees full of birds walking down to the water's edge,
Socrates in a basket hanging beside the full moon, eating a
    partridge,
The young men pushing, hubbub on Golgotha,
The mad king among them, terrified, smelling the sweat of the
    crowd,
Hegel arriving on a sea-scallop accompanied by Venus,—
All this I was, but also those four strangers
Leaning above me, leaning above the stream,
The tall man, the small man, and the blue-eyed woman,
And that other woman, whose beauty, on a kite,
Rose to a beauty like the evening star.
Golgotha, the skull, was the amphitheatre,
The skull was my skull, and within it played
The seven-man orchestra, while Luvic sang—

Lights! Lights! O'Dwyer hoarsely cried,
His bloodshot eyes peeped round the gilded smooth
Belly of a cherub, who supported
Chryselephantine pillar of fruits and lutes and leaves.
The lights changed, the walls
Came closer, the crowd was blue, obscure, the forest
Nodded, the blue smoke rolled among the leaves
And nests of birds. The orchestra sat playing

75

Typewriters, telephones and telegraphs
Under the calcium light
And on the stage red ropes had squared a ring.
Out of the forest flew the songs of birds,
While hid in leaves the saxophone made moan.
Bang! said the gong, and the red giant from his corner
Sprang to the ring, shaking the boards. The other
Rose terrified, submissive, his thin hands
Ungloved, his chin defenceless, and his heart
Visibly beating.

          'You! Narcissus!' I said!
And as I rose the giant's hard glove crashed
Black on the visible heart, and the sick man
Shot through the ropes and fell against the arch
Under the cherub at O'Dwyer's feet.

ONE TWO THREE FOUR FIVE
SIX SEVEN EIGHT NINE—
               the red hand
Counted, jerking. At the fatal nine
The sick man rose, crawled through the ropes, his face
White as a dead man's in the calcium light,
His dark eyes burning with fever, his weak hands
Uplifted, trembling.

          'You! Narcissus!' I said!
And saw again the hard black piston crash
Against the visible heart, and the sick man
Falling backward, on his back, in the dark corner,
Unconscious, motionless, his dark eyes
Wide open! Then the applause, roaring like rain!
The giant's bloody glove upheld! The gong clattering!
Bozo, Nozo, Glozo, the Tozos, cheering!
While from the forest blew a blast of sound,
Flutebirds and bubblebeaks, Harry and Tom,
The seven-man orchestra, the saxophone
Bubbling the *Himmelfahrt,* the Lo! the hero
Conquering comes!

          Lights! O'Dwyer rubbed
A bright alpaca sleeve across the cherub,

The forest darkened, the nodding lilies
Darkened also, the bare stage diminished,
Bozo, Nozo, Glozo, the Tozos, all were gone,
Only the half-dead man, who lay alone,
His white dead face propped up against the backdrop,
Staring, with dying eyes. To him I knelt,
While Doctor Wundt, above me, in a box,
Leaned down among the leaves
Pleasantly laughing, and that other man,
My father, chill from the grave, leaned down and smiled.
And it was then the blue-eyed woman triumphed
And glared with sovereign eye above the stream:
'What thinks he now? What peril seeks he now?
Digs now what magic?'

       'Digs in his heart a grave!'
Laughed Doctor Wundt. 'It is the half-dead man,
Himself, who longs to die; for him he digs.'

(It is true I ran to the dead man
And raised his head. Alas, what horror,
When I saw the chest-wall rotted, the heart
Hanging like a cluster of grapes,
Beating weakly, uncovered and sick.
Alas, too, what horror when he said:
Daily I fight here,
Daily I die for the world's delight
By the giant blow on my visible heart!)

Then from the wood arose a sigh of sound
Where lapped in leaves the seven-man orchestra,
Flutebird and bubblebeak, Harry and Tom,
Blew blue nostalgia out of 'Hearts and Flowers';
While Doctor Wundt, grown taller, and my father,
Flinging one haloed image on the stream,
Sang, with one voice, a mournful requiem.
'Inheritor!' This was the word they said,
But also sang, 'Alas, Narcissus dead,
Narcissus daily dead, that we may live!'

4

My father which art in earth
From whom I got my birth,
What is it that I inherit?
From the bones fallen apart
And the deciphered heart,
Body and spirit.

My mother which art in tomb
Who carriedst me in thy womb,
What is it that I inherit?
From the thought come to dust
And the remembered lust,
Body and spirit.

Father and mother, who gave
Life, love, and now the grave,
What is it that I can be?
Nothing but what lies here,
The hand still, the brain sere,
Naught lives in thee

Nor ever will live, save
It have within this grave
Roots in the mingled heart,
In the damp ashes wound
Where the past, underground,
Falls, falls apart.

The Coming Forth by Day of Osiris Jones

STAGE DIRECTIONS

It is a shabby backdrop of bright stars:
one of the small interstices of time:
the worn out north star northward, and Orion
to westward spread in ruined light. Eastward,
the other stars disposed,—or indisposed;—
x-ward or y-ward, the sick sun inflamed;
and all his drunken planets growing pale.
We watch them, and our watching is this hour.

It is a stage of ether, without space,—
a space of limbo without time,—
a faceless clock that never strikes;

and it is bloodstream at its priestlike task,—
the indeterminate and determined heart,
that beats, and beats, and does not know it beats.

Here the dark synapse between nerve and nerve;
the void, between two atoms in the brain;
darkness, without term or form, that sinks
between two thoughts.

              Here we have sounded, angel!—
O angel soul, O memory of man!—
and felt the nothing that sustains our wings.
And here have seen the catalogue of things—
all in the maelstrom of the limbo caught,
and whirled concentric to the funnel's end,
sans number, and sans meaning, and sans purpose;
save that the lack of purpose bears a name
the lack of meaning has a heart-beat, and
the lack of number wears a cloak of stars.

THE THINGS

The house in Broad Street, red brick, with nine rooms
the weedgrown graveyard with its rows of tombs
the jail from which imprisoned faces grinned
at stiff palmettos flashing in the wind

the engine-house, with engines, and a tank
in which young alligators swam and stank,
the bell-tower, of red iron, where the bell
gonged of the fires in a tone from hell

magnolia trees with whitehot torch of bud
the yellow river between banks of mud
the tall striped lighthouse like a barber's pole
snake in the bog and locust in the hole

worn cigarette cards, of white battleships,
or flags, or chorus girls with scarlet lips,
jackstones of copper, peach tree in the yard
splashing ripe peaches on an earth baked hard

children beneath the arc-light in a romp
with Run sheep Run, and rice-birds in the swamp,
the organ-grinder's monkey, dancing bears,
okras in baskets, Psyche on the stairs—

and then the north star nearer, and the snow
silent between the now and long ago
time like a train that roared from place to place
new crowds, new faces, for a single face

no longer then the chinaberry tree
nor the dark mockingbird to sing his glee
nor prawns nor catfish; icicles instead
and Indian-pipes, and cider in the shed

arbutus under pinewoods in the spring
and death remembered as a tropic thing

with picture postcard angels to upraise it
and trumpet vines and hummingbirds to phrase it

then wisdom come, and Shakspere's voice far off,
to be or not, upon the teacher's cough,
the latent heat of melting ice, the brief
hypotenuse from ecstasy to grief

amo amas, and then the *cras amet,*
the new-found eyes no slumber could forget,
Vivien, the affliction of the senses,
and conjugation of historic tenses

and Shakspere nearer come, and louder heard,
and the disparateness of flesh and word,
time growing swifter, and the pendulums
in shorter savage arcs that beat like drums—

hands held, relinquished, faces come and gone,
kissed and forgotten, and become but one,
old shoes worn out, and new ones bought, the gloves
soiled, and so lost in limbo, like the loves—

then Shakspere in the heart, the instant speech
parting the conscious terrors each from each—
wisdom's dishevelment, the purpose lamed,
and purposeless the footsteps eastward aimed

the bloodstream always slower, while the clock
followed the tired heart with louder knock,
fatigue upon the eye, the tardy springs
inviting to no longer longed-for things—

the birdsong nearer now than Shakspere's voice,
whispers of comfort—Death is near, rejoice!—
remember now the red house with nine rooms
the graveyard with its trumpetvines and tombs—

play jackstones now and let your jackstones be
the stars that make Orion's galaxy

so to deceive yourself until you move
into that house whose tenants do not love.

THE COSTUMES

Bought from an old clothes man who rang a bell
licence three hundred sixty-five, to sell

Item: a pair of infant's socks two inches long
a dozen diapers, a woolen shawl of blue
a linen dress embroidered by a spinster aunt
ditto, ditto, a bonnet of angora (ribbons for chin)
a pair of white kid shoes for dress occasions
a rubber sheet, a long cloak of white fur

Item: a dozen bibs, another dozen of diapers,
a pair of drawers made of thin rubber
a pair of woolen mittens
and a pair ditto of aluminum (perforated)
to prevent thumb-sucking

Item: a dozen pairs of shorts
shirts, stockings, sandals, and a sailor's cap

Item: six sailor blouses, with appropriate ties
anchors embroidered on sleeves, whistles attached by cords,
with short sailor trousers of serge
a black velvet jacket with trousers to match
neckties and various shoes

Item: long trousers
collar buttons, cufflinks of silver,
a large watch with a loud tick, much heard at night
a sweater, a woolen coat with brass buttons
and woolen gloves almost impervious to snowballs

Item: a dinner jacket, three stiff shirts, collars,
pumps for dancing, a derby hat,
a dress suit, white flannels, a bathing-suit,
a raincoat with plaid lining

Item: a pair of rubbers

Item: a pair of moccasins

Item: a tweed hat bought in England, green,
galoshes, silk shirts, collars of increasing sizes,
and assorted neckties, mostly blue

Item: pyjamas, linen for summer, woolen for winter
with tasseled cords and pockets in the jackets

Item: sundry felt hats

Item: a coffin.

CHARACTERISTIC COMMENTS

> *The nursery clock*
>   tick . . . tock
>
> *The face*
>   mmmmmmm . . . mmmmmmm
>
> *The sleeves*
>   put your arms in
>
> *The shoes*
>   don't break the laces
>
> *The handkerchief*
>   change me
>
> *The hat*
>   shape of your head
>
> *The necktie*
>   wrinkled
>
> *The fire*
>   your hands are cold

Shakspere
to lie in cold obstruction and to rot

Vivien
but Darling!

The rain
look at the streaked light on the window-pane

The other faces
we are smiling

The shoes
polish us

The pencils
sharpen us

The desk
work

The peach
eat me in sunlight

The prostitute
follow me

The coffin
I also serve who only lie in wait

The heart
I will

FOUR SPEECHES MADE BY AN OBELISK

North
Northward, the nothing that we give a name,
southward, the selfsame nothing without fame,
westward, the sunset over sterile sands
eastward, the stone Memnon with hollowed hands.

South
>Little is life, with love, or without love,
>with or without wings, bones can scarcely move,
>rain will destroy the flesh, the eyes go blind,
>and stone will not remember much the mind.

East
>Memorials erected by our slaves
>will close their eyes to time like humbler graves,
>Cheops and Jones indifferent grass will cover,
>the ant or worm will be the final lover.

West
>Speak if you will, it is as Memnon speaks
>of that supernal dawn that never breaks,
>or as I speak, on north south east and west
>of kings now useless who have gone to rest.

REMARKS ON THE PERSON OF MR. JONES

The trained nurse
>it's a fine boy, not a blemish, God bless him

The face
>mmmmmmmmmm . . . mmmmmmm

Other boys
>hey bricktop hey carrots

The teacher
>an appearance as of strength in reserve

The girl
>who let you out? are you wet behind the ears?

The music
>your heart is beating, your will is strong
>you are walking in a hall of clouds
>your hand is cunning and the gods are young

Picture of a mountain
    you too

The horses in the field
    you are swift

The leaf
    you are brief

The snow
    centuries hence, it will be long ago

The mirror
    lights, lights, more lights!

Memory
    this is a roiled reflection of the face

Vivien
    If you had wings you would be less an angel
    and more the devil that you sometimes are
    but you're an angel and a devil, too
    and amateur at both

Pride
    Look at that biceps! measure it with your hand.
    Was ever such a consciousness as this?
    here's wisdom that would break behemoth's heart
    and such a passion as could shape the world
    to better purpose

Shame
    Foulest, foulest, foulest,
    digester of filth, excreter of filth,
    unwashed effluvium of this rotting world,
    sickly beginning and more sickly end,
    cut out that natural heart that beats your blood
    and with it shed your life

The sun
    rejoice

86

The rain
weep

INSCRIPTIONS IN SUNDRY PLACES

On a billboard
smoke Sweet Caporals

In a street-car
do not speak to the motorman

On a vending machine
insert one cent then press the rod
push push push push

On a weighing machine
give yourself a weigh

On the schoolhouse
Morton Grammar School Founded 1886

In gilt letters on a swinging black sign
Dr. William F. Jones M.D.

On a tombstone
memento mori

On a coin
e pluribus unum

On the fence of a vacant lot
commit no nuisance

In a library
silence

At the entrance to a graveyard
dogs admitted only on leash

At a zoo
do not feed the animals

On a cotton wharf
　　no smoking

On a crocheted bookmarker in a Bible
　　time is short

On a sailor cap
　　U. S. S. Oregon

At a railway-crossing
　　stop look and listen

At the end of a road
　　private way dangerous passing

Beside a pond
　　no fishing

In a park
　　keep off the grass

In a train
　　spitting prohibited $100 fine

On a celluloid button
　　remember the Maine

On a brick wall
　　trespassers will be prosecuted to the full extent of the law

Outside a theatre
　　standing room only

At the foot of a companionway leading to the bridge of a ship
　　officers only

In a subway
　　the cough and sneeze
　　both spread disease
　　and so does spit
　　take care of it

Over the gateway to a college yard
  What is man that thou art mindful of him?

Ditto
  enter to grow in wisdom

On a sign hung with two lanterns beside a frozen river
  no skating

Beside a wood
  no shooting

Behind a building in a dark alley
  No sir, carry your water up the street

In a public lavatory
  fools' names and fools' faces
  always show in public places
  and this I'll add if you don't know it
  that Shakespere was no backhouse poet

Ditto
  Mabel Waters 26 John Street

Ditto
  do not deface

Ditto
  say when you'll meet me

Ditto
  it was down in the Lehigh Valley—me and my saucy Sue

In a museum
  visitors are requested not to touch the objects

In a concert hall
  no admission after doors are closed

On an office door
    Peter Jones

In a saloon
    no treating allowed

Laundry-mark on linen
    B69

In a window
    board and room

On a ship
    first class passengers not allowed aft of this sign

In a train
    ne pas se pencher au dehors

On an apartment-house door
    all deliveries must be made at side entrance

Over a door in a hospital
    staff only

VARIOUS ROOMS

The nursery
    High on the southern wall the clock
    tick—tock—tick—tock—
    and on the western wall the rain
    flashing claws on the window pane
    the ceiling white the walls blue
    the shawl above you is blue too
    here is the place where comes the face
    and murmurs mmmmmm—mmmmmm.

    The walls are changed and papered well
    with peacock and red tulip bell
    here is a desk with pen and ink
    and here at night you sit and think

of Jesus and the Holy Ghost
the fisherman whose wife was lost
the genii in the bottle, and
Julius Caesar and fairyland
and two plus two and four plus four
and footsteps pause behind the door—

The dining-room
    Porridge and cream for breakfast, sugar-bowls,
    soft bibs and soft-boiled eggs, and salt-cellars
    of crusted silver, tiny silver spoons,
    the chandelier that fell, the silver bell,
    nasturtiums in a cut-glass bowl that sparkled.

The hall
    here once was Waterloo, and here the great
    Napoleon deployed a hundred tents;
    and cannons shot dried peas against the wall.

Father's office
    a verb is an action being or state of being;
    the articles are 'the' and 'an' or 'a';
    around the rugged rock the ragged rascal ran

The schoolroom
    these desks, all carved with names, once saw him rise
    and in his trouser-pocket put the prize

Kitchen
    tin mug of coffee on an oilcloth table;
    advertisements of pills for female ills

Sunday school
    the fatherhood of God, the brotherhood of man—

Another schoolroom
    let me see that paper. Did you cheat?

A room in a school hospital
    so the three caravels to westward veiling

foamworthy frows and able seamnen seething
southward in soft altlantic saw you sinking
depe depe and deeper darkly down and drown
drenched and despatched and drunk with more than ether
ceiling concentric to a funnel flaring
sounds of wide froth and sea-surge softly hearing
whispers of space and time and nothing caring
the silver bubbles blinkt and you an oyster
dark smells of oakum, far above three shadows
Columbus gone, America discovered
down drown down drown down drown and you too soon
for what you know already and forget
put up your hands and touch the keels Columbus

A lecture-room
Focus a little experience—

A bedroom
Quick—stand behind the door—don't make a sound
don't breathe. Sorry the towels are so dirty.
When you go down, carry your shoes in your hand!

Another bedroom
Darling darling darling darling darling

Another bedroom
It's only a handkerchief—see?
I've got the flowers. Honest I didn't know it.

Another bedroom
Give me another sovereign and I will

Another bedroom
I never knew, I never knew.
I didn't either.
Look—it's beginning to snow.
Perhaps you'd better close the window, do you think?

An office
Well, I'll meet you half way

Another bedroom
>Is that you Vivien?
>This is the face I saw, this is the face
>the trumpetvine the tombstone and the place
>This is what music said
>look, you are walking in a hall of clouds
>your hand is cunning, the gods are young

A drawing-room
>Lovely weather isn't it? How do you do

A ballroom
>One, two, three-and-slide; one, two, three-and-slide;
>down by the stream where I first met Rebecca

An office
>In reply to your inquiry of the 16th instant—

A stateroom
>Creak—and a wash of sea—bells and a bugle,
>the north star drowned, a majesty of waves
>washing the heart, and memory but a night
>in which at last a single face is bright

Bedroom in a hospital
>Now if you'll roll your sleeve up, I will give you
>this little shot of morphine, which will help you
>you'll be surprised, it will be very easy
>lie still and close our eyes.

MR. JONES ADDRESSES A LOOKING-GLASS

Mr. Jones
>So this is you

The mirror
>yes this is me

Mr. Jones
>but I am more
>than what I see

The mirror
>what are you then
>if more than that?
>a coat a collar
>and a hat

Mr. Jones
>also a heart
>also a soul
>also a will
>that knows its goal

The mirror
>you are a razor
>in a claw
>and more than that
>I never saw

Mr. Jones
>far more than that
>I am a mind
>whose wanderings
>are unconfined
>north south and east
>and west I go
>and all things under god
>I know

The mirror
>speak if you must
>but I distrust
>and all that glitters
>is but dust

Mr. Jones
>but I remember
>what I see

and that, in mirrors,
cannot be

The mirror
  well, Mr. Jones, perhaps it's better
  to be, like me, a good forgetter

Mr. Jones
  how can you know what here goes on
  behind this flesh-bright frontal bone?
  here are the world and god, become
  for all their depth a simple *Sum.*

The mirror
  well, keep the change, then, Mr. Jones,
  and, if you can, keep brains and bones,
  but as for me I'd rather be
  unconscious, except when I see.

THE FACE

The blue shawl first, a canopy of blue,
blue sky, blue ceiling, the bewildering light
that comes and goes, and in it formless forms
and then the form of forms the shape of shapes
the darkness with the face, the face with eyes,
the face with stars, the leaning face, the murmur,

sweet food, sweet softness, incalculable depth
unassailable but protective height
the tower among the stars, great Igdrasil,
and so the sounds grown slower, more distinct,
one from another clear, the murmur shaking
deeply the chords of being, and the voice

speaking or singing, with notes far apart—
so far apart that terror folds his wings
between one syllable of sweetest sound

and its successor,—but so slow, so slow,
that terror downward, on delicious wings,
floats,—falls in the darkness,—in the silence,—

then upward beats his wings, when the word sings,
is gone away, into the blue of heaven,
up to the shawl of stars—and here the instant voice
murmurs into the heart, into the throat,
till all the blood is radiant in the veins
whispers the secret, the lost secret, far away

and it is bird song, it is boughs of trees,
the flight of light among palmetto leaves,
the wave of wind across the field of daisies,
the voice of water fluctuant in the night,
and the street-vendor, the old negress, singing
'yea, prawns, yea, okras,' in the bright blue morning—

and then the face withdrawn, farther withdrawn,
into the sunset red behind the lighthouse,
beyond the river's mouth, beyond the marsh,
far out at sea, or stars between two clouds,
farther and farther, till it lives again
only in nearer things—and it is now

the sunlight on the hand and on cold grass,
the acorn cup half filled with rain, the locust
unfolding irised wings of isinglass
the hummingbird above the flower's mouth
on an invisible cord of purest gold—
wing shadows on the wall of an old house—

and now in speed recaptured, now in strength,
and now in words dissembled, or half seen,
as when strange syllables with sudden brightness
open dark eyes, and all the page of words
becomes a field of flowers, moving and fragrant,
clover and tulip in deep grass and leaves—

all stirred and stirring in a wind from somewhere
far off and half remembered—from that sky,

that ceiling, that bewildering light, that shawl
of stars from which the voice of voices came;
then lost once more, and half seen farther on,
glimpsed in the lightning, heard in a peal of thunder—

diffused, and more diffused, till music speaks
under a hundred lights, with violins,
soft horns, nostalgic oboes, where again
the terror comes between one sound and other,
floats,—falls in the darkness,—in the silence,—
then upward beats his wings when the voice sings—

and it is life, but it is also death,
it is the whisper of the always lost
but always known, it is the first and last
of heaven's light, the end and the beginning,
follows the moving memory like a shadow,
and only rests, at last, when that too comes to rest.

UNOFFICIAL REPORT MADE BY DIVERS TRYSTING PLACES

A *lamp-post*
> He stood here. It was the hour of the dog.
> His hat pulled down to shield his face,
> his dirty raincoat on his arm, his hand
> holding his watch.

Bench in an avenue
> He sat here, in the dark, watching the cars
> feel through the night-fog with long bright antennae
> then rose, walked off a little, and came back,
> and sat and rose again. Then Vivien came—
> Vivien and the infinite togehter!
> St. Mary's rang the angelus in the fog.
> I heard them laughing as he took her hand,
> and the night swallowed them.

Library in a hotel
> The prostitute sat here beside the table.

He was late: he kept her waiting.
She was pale, her dress was shabby,
she smoked three cigarettes, crossed, and uncrossed her knees,
looked at her wrist watch, angrily,
and read a magazine of Christian Science.
When he came, they scarcely spoke.

Entrance to a subway
>He waited almost an hour, in the snow;
>but no one came.

Lobby of a hotel
>Every Wednesday, at two o'clock
>he stood here, smoking, waiting;
>he called her Gwen.

A tree on a hill
>Three times he met his Vivien here:
>three times I gave them blessing.

A park bench
>It was the hour of Venus and the sailor.
>They sat here eating popcorn. She was a Jewess.
>The arc-light, shining through the cottonwood,
>showed trampled mud and peanut shells
>and a discarded garter. The swans were asleep,
>dead matches floated in the dirty water,
>and the gardens filled with whispered laughter.
>Afterwards, when they smoked,
>she laughed, and said she had a son in Troy.

A lamp-post
>He stood here. It was the hour of the wolf,
>his hat pulled down, his raincoat on;
>but when she came, it was a different girl.

Bench in an avenue
>They quarreled here. He rose and walked away.
>She sat here crying.

Entrance to a subway
      He stood beside his suitcase, reading a paper.
      When they met, they were both embarrassed.

A tree on a hill
      They will remember me.

Bench in an avenue
      For many days she came and sat alone.

Lobby of a dingy hotel
      I knew him well.

REPORT MADE BY A MEDICAL STUDENT
TO WHOM WAS ASSIGNED FOR INSPECTION
THE CASE OF MR. JONES

Facies
      sallow and somewhat haggard; thin and pallid;
      intelligent; with no marked cyanosis;
      the lips however pale and slightly blueish.
      No prominent veins, no jaundice, no oedema.
      The eyes are sunken, broad dark rings around them;
      conjunctivae, pale; gums, not affected;
      no blue line, and no sponginess. Tongue,—moist;
      with yellow coat . . . The right ear shows
      a small herpetic cluster on the lobule.

Neck
      no enlargement; normal pulsation.

Chest
      as a whole, symmetrical in outline.
      respiratory movements, uniform.
      Supra-clavicular (and infra-clavicular) regions
      no more depressed than anaemia warrants.
      No heart-impulse visible. Apex beat not seen.

Abdomen

> the skin, deeply pigmented. The abdomen
> somewhat distended; uniform in shape.
> Found only one small spot that might be thought
> a rose-spot: no abdominal pulsation.

Extremities

> forearms and thighs, dotted with small spots—
> average about a pinhead size (some larger)—
> varying from the color of fresh blood
> to almost black. Are not removed by pressure,—
> not raised above the surface, sharply outlined:
> appear (on close inspection) as minute
> haemorrhages beneath the epidermis . . .
> The skin, harsh, scaly. Follicles, not prominent.
> Muscles, somewhat flaccid. No oedema.

Palpation

> confirmed throughout the character of the skin.
> No evidence of enlarged glands on the neck.
> None found in the groin or the axillae.
> The heart impulse not felt; nor apex beat.
> Could not determine lower border of liver.
> Over a considerable area, and bilateral,
> marked tenderness, most marked in lower portion.
> Recti contracted—spasmodically—under pressure.

Percussion

> the lungs gave normal resonance throughout.
> The area of cardiac dulness
> came half an inch within the mammary line.
> The abdomen, throughout, was tympanitic,—
> flat on the flanks well back; dull on the pubes;—
> which I attribute to contracted recti.
> The upper limit of the negative dulness
> was opposite fifth rib in mammary line.
> Flatness began at sixth rib. Lower border
> seemed normal in position. Splenic enlargement
> could not be well determined; normal dulness
> not easily distinguished, partly owing
> to tympany of stomach and intestines.

Auscultation
negative as regards the chest; nothing abnormal
was audible in either lung.
The apex beat was heard (equally well)
in interspaces four and five.
The heart-sounds feeble: difficult to hear;
the first sound, valvular; the second, clicking.
No murmur. In the neck, no venous hum.
No friction sounds were heard above the liver.
Did not examine spleen for friction sounds.

The eruption
first noticed with the first abdominal pains.
On radial side of forearm, near the wrist,
a bruise-like spot, size of a dime;
which passed through various shades of red and blue;
then brown and black; scaled off; and disappeared.

SPEECHES MADE BY BOOKS, STARS, THINGS AND PEOPLE

The books
Everyman I will go with thee and be thy guide,
in thy most need
to go by thy side.

The people
Hi there Jones
say did you mean that?
well, telling him won't make him, will it
when I saw you you were sitting at the café table, thinking

The stars
Look at us

Shakspere
And death being dead there's no more dying then

The people
Hi there Jones!

The stars
>Light-years!

The books
>Homage to thee, o great God, lord of truth.
>O lord I come to thee to see thy kindness
>I know thee and I know thy name, and know
>the names of all those gods who dwell with thee.

The people
>He must go westward to the outer darkness
>and die, and pick the deathless asphodels.

The stars
>We are eyes

The books
>Behold I have come to thee, and I bring truth
>sin I destroyed for thee, I have not sinned
>against mankind, nor yet against my kin
>nor wronged the place of truth, nor known the worthless.
>I wrought no evil, nor cheated the oppressed,
>nor did those things the gods abominate
>nor vilified the servant to his lord.

The people
>He's a liar.

The stars
>Winter is coming.

The books
>Never have I caused pain, nor let man hunger
>made man or woman weep, nor children weep,
>have not committed murder, nor commanded
>others to do my murder. I have not
>stolen the offerings to departed spirits
>nor robbed the gods of their oblations, nor
>committed fornication.

The people
>Hey bricktop hey carrots
>who let you out? are you wet behind the ears?
>his hands are covered with blood.

The stars
>Nebular hypothesis.

The books
>Have not polluted myself in holy places
>diminished from the bushel, taken from
>nor added to the acre-measure, nor
>encroached on fields of others. Nor have I
>misread the pointers of the scales, nor added weight,
>I have not taken milk from mouths of children,
>nor caught the fish with fish of their own kind.

The people
>The sycamores will have no food for this guy
>he lies in his throat
>lynch him

The stars
>Square of the distance?

The books
>I have not put out a fire when it should burn
>I have not driven cattle from their pastures
>I have not cut the dam of a canal
>I have not shunned the god at his appearance
>I am pure. I am pure. I am pure. I am pure. I am pure.

The people
>Outside, outside!
>close the door after you, will you?
>who let him in anyway?
>hi there Jones

The pendulums
>Pain—pang—pain—pang—pain—pang.

The stars
> First degree! second degree! third degree! forever.

The things
> We know better

A clock
> Cuckoo! cuckoo! cuckoo!

The beds
> Foul enseamèd sheets

A girl
> Hello Peter—do you remember me?

A dollar-bill
> He'd steal a penny from a dead man's eye

A grave
> Enter, to grow in wisdom

A cat
> He kicked me

The peach-tree
> He broke me

Waste-basket
> Filled me with circulars and unpaid bills

The hands of a clock
> Here we go round the mulberry bush
> mulberry bush mulberry bush

Jackstone
> I am still here in the yard, under a brick

Psyche
> He drew a moustache on me with an indelible pencil

The locusts
   Look out for the wasps

The swamp
   Beware the snake

The books
   Homage to you who dwell in the hall of truth
   I know you and I know your names. Let me not fall
   under the slaughtering knives, bring not my wickedness
   to the notice of the god whom you all follow;
   speak ye the truth concerning me to god.
   I have not done an evil thing, but live
   on truth, and feed on truth, and have performed
   behests of men, and things that please the gods.

The things
   Pull out the plug.

Broad street
   Hot asphalt!

Ricebirds in the swamp
   Gunshot!

The organ
   Please give a penny to the poor blind man—
   poor blind man—poor blind man—

Shakspere
   Walk you thus westward you will see the west
   grown colder but still west: or march you east
   why eastward still the sun will blanch before you,
   with ice upon his eyes, but still the sun.

Picture-postcard angels
   Harp the herald tribune sings

The music
   Angel of nothing in a world of nothings,
   palmetto leaf in sunlight, time and tide

divinely moving, and the lighthouse bright
against the golden western sunset light—
O phrase of beauty, in the darkness born,
spoken and stilled; swiftness against the cloud;
cloud against starlight, heartbeat in the blood,
memory of the dust and gods of dust:
weak hand that touched, strong hand that held, weak hand
    that touched,
eyes that forgetting saw, and saw recalling,
and saw again forgetting; memory moving
from wonder to disaster, and to wonder,
the bloodstream full of twilight, and the twilight
inflamed with sunsets of remembered birth;
O death, in shape of change, in shape of time,
in flash of leaf and murmur, delighting god
whose godhead is a vapour, whose delight
is icicles in summer, and arbutus
under the snowdrift, and the river flowing
westward among the reeds and flying birds
beyond the obelisks and hieroglyphs—
whisper of whence and why, question in darkness
answered in silence, but such silence, angel,
as answers only gods who seek for gods—
rejoice, for we are come to such a world
as no thought sounded.

The desk

    I'll meet you half way, he said.
    I'll meet you half way, he said.
    I'll meet you half way, he said.

The people

    Hi there Jones.
    where's your bankbook?
    well, he's a good egg, at that.

Vivien

    If I were less the face and more myself
    if you were less the face and more yourself
    if we were less the face and more ourselves
    and time turned backward, but our knowledge kept—

The operating-table
    Now if you'll roll your sleeve up I will give you—

The stars
    Open your mouth and shut your eyes—
    and I will give you a great surprise.
    Eclipse
    obscuration
    transit
A basket of okras
    Childhood! sunshine!

The shoes
    Laces broken, worn out

The books
    I gave a boat to him who needed one.
    I have made holy offerings to the gods.
    Be ye my saviours, be ye my protectors,
    and make no accusations before God.
    Look, I am pure of mouth, and clean of hands,
    therefore it hath been said by those who saw me
    come in peace, come in peace, come in peace.

The graveyard
    Come to pieces! bones to you, old bonetrap

The snow
    Poor Pete's a-cold

The books
    My heart of my mother—my heart of my mother—my heart
        of my being,—
    make no stand against me when testifying,—
    thrust me not back to darkness!

The face
    My little son!

Truth
>Tell me: who is he whose roof is fire,
>whose walls are living serpents, and whose floor
>a stream of water?

Hypotenuse
>The shortest distance—ha ha—between two points

The people
>Dirty dog—!
>look at the cut of his trousers.
>Hi there Jones!

The books
>In very truth this heart has now been weighed
>this soul born testimony concerning him
>this that comes from his mouth has been confirmed
>he has not sinned, his name stinks not before us
>let him go forth into the field of flowers
>let him go forth into the field of offerings
>let him go forth into the field of reeds.

The people
>Bribery! simony! perjury! blasphemy!

The stars
>Chaos—hurray!—is come again

The face
>Divinest of divine and love of loves
>daybreak of brightest light and morning star
>murmur of music in the fairest flower
>o cloven sweetest fruit, and tenderest vine
>dear timelessness of time and heavenly face
>and dearest clover in the darkest place—

A lamp-post
>Here he spat

A document
    Here is his name, perjured

A ditch
    Here he stooped

The face
    Wonder of wonders in a world of worlds
    o heart that beats beneath a larger heart
    quick hands to beauty born in helplessness
    and love of loveliness with tenderest touch—

The stars
    Great Circle

The outer darkness
    Airless! Waterless! Lightless!

The books
    In god's name, and god's image, let him die

The clock
    Tock.

LANDSCAPE WITH FIGURES

The birches
    tell the tale silverly

The larches
    whisper it—hush

The pines
    who was it? who?

The junipers
    the bird in the bush

The brook
>Demosthenes' pebbles

The wind
>where was it? when?

The grass
>she? who was she?

The echo
>tell it again

The hillside
>warm sun upon these frozen bones of granite—
>I stretched my ribs and thawed—

The haunted house
>another frost like that, the chimney'll fall—
>there was ice by the pond's edge.

The cricket
>zeek . . . zeek . . . zeek

The wind
>who did you say she was? who?

The brook
>she babbled, she laughed, half weeping she loitered,
>she laughed without laughter, wept without tearfall—

The echo
>laughed and laughed laughed and laughed

The wind
>why did she? where? . . .

The pines
>seek her and soothe her!

The birches
> tale-telling tell-tale!
> this frost makes me tinkle.

The cricket
> seek . . . seek . . . seek . . . seek . . .

The hillside
> slowly the hard earth, from these cusps of granite
> softly in sunlight released—

The bell-tower
> doomed in hell, domed in hell, doomed.

The brook
> she, she was querulous:
> he, he was quarrelsome:

The echo
> he he!—she she!

The haunted house
> alas, alas how this cold autumn-wind
> moans through old rib-bones! whines through old clapboards!

The grass
> they? who were they? . . .
> sure, surely I saw them . . .

The pines
> who saw them? you?

The brook
> babblers and wind-bibblers
> leave love alone!

The echo
> fling the first stone

The brook
  wept she then? walked she then? whither.

The hillside
  warm sun upon these frosted bones of granite—
  I stretch my ribs and thaw beneath the lichens—
  the drip from hoarfrost tickles at my sides
  and runs toward that chattering brook—

The haunted house
  I knew it—that brick at the top is loose.

The cricket
  seek . . . see . . . seek . . . see . . .

The bell-tower
  doom doing, doomsday, doom done, doom.

The larches
  where are they vanished to?

The brook
  what was that word that so hurt her? what hurt her so?

The birches
  whisper it

The larches
  soothesay

The pines
  where and when? who and why?

The grass
  shhhhhhhhh! . . . shhhhhhh!

Preludes for Memnon
OR
PRELUDES TO ATTITUDE

I

Winter for a moment takes the mind; the snow
Falls past the arclight; icicles guard a wall;
The wind moans through a crack in the window;
A keen sparkle of frost is on the sill.
Only for a moment; as spring too might engage it,
With a single crocus in the loam, or a pair of birds;
Or summer with hot grass; or autumn with a yellow leaf.
Winter is there, outside, is here in me:
Drapes the planets with snow, deepens the ice on the moon,
Darkens the darkness that was already darkness.
The mind too has its snows, its slippery paths,
Walls bayonetted with ice, leaves ice-encased.
Here is the in-drawn room, to which you return
When the wind blows from Arcturus: here is the fire
At which you warm your hands and glaze your eyes;
The piano, on which you touch the cold treble;
Five notes like breaking icicles; and then silence.

The alarm-clock ticks, the pulse keeps time with it,
Night and the mind are full of sounds. I walk
From the fire-place, with its imaginary fire,
To the window, with its imaginary view.
Darkness, and snow ticking the window: silence,
And the knocking of chains on a motor-car, the tolling
Of a bronze bell, dedicated to Christ.
And then the uprush of angelic wings, the beating
Of wings demonic, from the abyss of the mind:
The darkness filled with a feathery whistling, wings

Numberless as the flakes of angelic snow,
The deep void swarming with wings and sound of wings,
The winnowing of chaos, the aliveness
Of depth and depth and depth dedicated to death.

Here are the bickerings of the inconsequential,
The chatterings of the ridiculous, the iterations
Of the meaningless. Memory, like a juggler,
Tosses its colored balls into the light, and again
Receives them into darkness. Here is the absurd,
Grinning like an idiot, and the omnivorous quotidian,
Which will have its day. A handful of coins,
Tickets, items from the news, a soiled handkerchief,
A letter to be answered, notice of a telephone call,
The petal of a flower in a volume of Shakspere,
The program of a concert. The photograph, too,
Propped on the mantel, and beneath it a dry rosebud;
The laundry bill, matches, an ash-tray, Utamaro's
Pearl-fishers. And the rug, on which are still the crumbs
Of yesterday's feast. These are the void, the night,
And the angelic wings that make it sound.

What is the flower? It is not a sigh of color,
Suspiration of purple, sibilation of saffron,
Nor aureate exhalation from the tomb.
Yet it is these because you think of these,
An emanation of emanations, fragile
As light, or glisten, or gleam, or coruscation,
Creature of brightness, and as brightness brief.
What is the frost? It is not the sparkle of death,
The flash of time's wing, seeds of eternity;
Yet it is these because you think of these.
And you, because you think of these, are both
Frost and flower, the bright ambiguous syllable
Of which the meaning is both no and yes.

Here is the tragic, the distorting mirror
In which your gesture becomes grandiose;
Tears form and fall from your magnificent eyes,
The brow is noble, and the mouth is God's.
Here is the God who seeks his mother, Chaos,—

Confusion seeking solution, and life seeking death.
Here is the rose that woos the icicle; the icicle
That woos the rose. Here is the silence of silences
Which dreams of becoming a sound, and the sound
Which will perfect itself in silence. And all
These things are only the uprush from the void,
The wings angelic and demonic, the sound of the abyss
Dedicated to death. And this is you.

II

Two coffees in the Español, the last
Bright drops of golden Barsac in a goblet,
Fig paste and candied nuts . . . Hardy is dead,
And James and Conrad dead, and Shakspere dead,
And old Moore ripens for an obscene grave,
And Yeats for an arid one; and I, and you—
What winding sheet for us, what boards and bricks,
What mummeries, candles, prayers, and pious frauds?
You shall be lapped in Syrian scarlet, woman,
And wear your pearls, and your bright bracelets, too,
Your agate ring, and round your neck shall hang
Your dark blue lapis with its specks of gold.
And I, beside you—ah! but will that be?
For there are dark streams in this dark world, lady,
Gulf Streams and Arctic currents of the soul;
And I may be, before our consummation
Beds us together, cheek by jowl, in earth,
Swept to another shore, where my white bones
Will lie unhonored, or defiled by gulls.

What dignity can death bestow on us,
Who kiss beneath a streetlamp, or hold hands
Half hidden in a taxi, or replete
With coffee, figs and Barsac make our way
To a dark bedroom in a wormworn house?
The aspidistra guards the door; we enter,
Per aspidistra—then—*ad astra*—is it?—
And lock ourselves securely in our gloom
And loose ourselves from terror. . . . Here's my hand,
The white scar on my thumb, and here's my mouth

To stop your murmur; speechless let us lie,
And think of Hardy, Shakspere, Yeats and James;
Comfort our panic hearts with magic names;
Stare at the ceiling, where the taxi lamps
Make ghosts of light; and see, beyond this bed,
That other bed in which we will not move;
And, whether joined or separated, will not love.

III

Sleep: and between the closed eyelids of sleep,
From the dark spirit's still unresting grief,
The one tear burns its way. O God, O God,
What monstrous world is this, whence no escape
Even in sleep? Between the fast-shut lids
This one tear comes, hangs on the lashes, falls:
Symbol of some gigantic dream, that shakes
The secret-sleeping soul . . . And I descend
By a green cliff that fronts the worldlong sea;
Disastrous shore; where bones of ships and rocks
Are mixed; and beating waves bring in the sails
Of unskilled mariners, ill-starred. The gulls
Fall in a cloud upon foul flotsam there;
The air resounds with cries of scavengers.

Dream: and between the close-locked lids of dream
The terrible infinite intrudes its blue:
Ice: silence: death the abyss of Nothing.
O God, O God, let the sore soul have peace.
Deliver it from this bondage of harsh dreams.
Release this shadow from its object, this object
From its shadow. Let the fleet soul go nimbly,—
Down,—down,—from step to step of dark,—
From dark to deeper dark, from dark to rest.
And let no Theseus-thread of memory
Shine in that labyrinth, or on those stairs,
To guide her back; nor bring her, where she lies,
Remembrance of a torn world well forgot.

VII

Beloved, let us once more praise the rain.
Let us discover some new alphabet,
For this, the often-praised; and be ourselves
The rain, the chickweed, and the burdock leaf,
The green-white privet flower, the spotted stone,
And all that welcomes rain; the sparrow, too,—
Who watches with a hard eye, from seclusion,
Beneath the elm-tree bough, till rain is done.

There is an oriole who, upside down,
Hangs at his nest, and flicks an orange wing,—
Under a tree as dead and still as lead;
There is a single leaf, in all this heaven
Of leaves, which rain has loosened from its twig:
The stem breaks, and it falls, but it is caught
Upon a sister leaf, and thus she hangs;
There is an acorn cup, beside a mushroom,
Which catches three drops from the stooping cloud.

The timid bee goes back to hive; the fly
Under the broad leaf of the hollyhock
Perpends stupid with cold; the raindark snail
Surveys the wet world from a watery stone . . .
And still the syllables of water whisper:
The wheel of cloud whirs slowly: while we wait
In the dark room; and in your heart I find
One silver raindrop,—on a hawthorn leaf,—
Orion in a cobweb, and the World.

VIII

Conceive: be fecundated by the word.
Hang up your mind for the intrusion of the wind.
Be blown, be blown, like a handful of withered seed,
Or a handful of leaves in autumn. Blow, blow,
Careless of where you blow, or to what end,
Or whether living or dying. Go with the wind,
Whirl and return, lodge in a tree, detach,

Sail on a stream in scarlet for trout to stare at,
Comfortless, aimless, brilliant. There is nothing
So suits the soul as change.

You have no name:
And what you call yourself is but a whisper
Of that divine and deathless and empty word
Which breathed all things to motion. You are *you*?
But what is you? What is this thing called you?
A seed, a leaf? a singing congregation
Of molecules? an atom split in two?
Electrons dancing in a magic circle?
A world, of which self-knowledge is the centre?
Laugh, and forget yourself; despise, and change
Hate, or do murder, love, beget, despair.
Go down and up again, go in and out,
Drink of the black and bright, bathe in the bitter,
Burn in the fiercest, and be light as ash.

You might have been a sparkle of clear sand.
You, who remember for a twinkling instant
All things, or what you think all things to be,
Whose cries consume you, or whose joys
Hoist you to heaven, such heaven as you will:
You might have been a dream dreamed in a dream
By some one dreaming of God and dreamed by God.
You might indeed have been a God, a star,
A world of stars and Gods, a web of time;
You might have been the word that breathed the world.

You are all things, and nothing. Ah poor being,
Sad ghost of wind, dead leaf of autumnal God,
Bright seed of brief disaster, changing shape:
Go with the wind, be untenacious, yet
Tenacious too; touch quickly what you may;
Remember and forget; and all transact
As if each touch were fatal and the last.
You are all things, and all things are your soul.

X

But you and I, Charybdis, are not new;
And all that flows between us is the dead . . .
—Thus Scylla, the scarred rock, sad child of time,
Benumbed with barnacles and hung with weed,
With urchins at her feet, and on her brow
Foul nests of cormorants, addressed her moan
To hear Charybdis, who, beyond the whirlpool,
Lifted a hornèd crag to God and Nothing.
And still the salt sea sucked between them, bearing
The bones of ships and bones of humans, white
The one as other, and as little worth.

Where is this corner of the crumbling world:
Where are these rocks, beloved, that cry out
Their hate and fear of time, their bitter sadness
At past, and passing, and the sense of past?
It is between ourselves these waters flow.
It is ourselves who are these self-same rocks,—
And we it is whom time has cracked and hung
With frost and filth. The sea-gull's is our voice;
The wail of mariners; the cry of wind.
And all that flows between us is the dead.

No need to go to Lethe, nor to Sibyl,
To memory, or forgetfulness, or both,
To find such horror, or such richness, mixed,
As we can find who smile here face to face.
The waters of the human soul are deep.
We are the rocks that rot above those waters.
We are the rocks on whom the times have written.
We, the recorded sadness of the world.

What marvels, then, for us, who know already
All that the waters of the godhead give?
Let us desist from this forlorn attempt
To wring strange beauty from a world well known.
Patience is all: so Shakspere might have said.

Let us be patient, then, and hear at night
The flux and reflux of the whirlpool, borne
Restless between us; submit, since needs we must,
To sad remembrance; but remember also
That there was nought before remembrance was.

XIII

And how begin, when there is no beginning?
How end, when there's no ending? How cut off
One drop of blood from other, break the stream
Which, with such subtlety, such magnificent power,
Binds the vast windflower to its throbbing world?
. . . Shall we be bold, and say, then, 'at this point
The world begins, the windflower ends'? rip out
One bleeding atom, pretend it has no kin? . . .
Or shall we, with the powerful mind, hold off
The sky from earth, the earth from sky, to see
Each perish into nothing?

            They will perish:
The drop of blood, the windflower, and the world;
Sound will be silence; meaning will have no meaning.
The blade of grass, in such a light, will grow
Monstrous as Minotaur; the tick of the clock,—
Should it be taken as the clock's dark secret,—
Is chaos and catastrophe; the heart
Cries like a portent in a world of portents,
All meaningless and mad.

            Softly, together,
We tread our little arcs upon our star;
Stare at each other's eyes, and see them thinking;
Lay hands upon our hearts and feel them beating;
But what precedes the luminous thought, or what
Unnumbered heartbeats timed the beat we feel,—
What burnings up of suns, or deaths of moons,
Shaped them, or what wreckage in time's stream,—
Ignore . . . And are our footsteps parallel?
Or runs your blood as slow as mine? or comes
The golden crocus, of this April's fiction,

As hotly to your thought as mine? The birds
That throng imagination's boughs, and sing,
Or flash from sward to leaf, for the sheer joy
Of mounting or descending in thought's air;
Or mate in ecstasy, and from that flame
Breed constellations of flame-colored flight:
Come they and go they, love, in your green tree
As swiftly as in mine? was there such singing
In mine as yours, or at the self-same season?
Have I such boughs as you, in the same place;
Or such a surf of leaves, when the wind blows;
Or such a fountain of bright flame, when birds
All skyward mount together?—

                  So we pace
From here to there, from there to here,—touch hands
As alien each to each as leaf and stone,
One chaos and another. Have good heart!
Your chaos is my world; perhaps my chaos
Is world enough for you. For what's unguessed
Will have such shape and sweetness as the knowing
Ruins with pour of knowledge. From one bird
We guess the tree, and hear the song; but if
Miraculous vision gives us, all at once,
The universe of birds and boughs, and all
The trees and birds from which their time has come,—
The world is lost. . .
           Love, let us rest in this.

XIV

—You went to the verge, you say, and come back safely?
Some have not been so fortunate,—some have fallen.
Children go lightly there, from crag to crag,
And coign to coign,—where even the goat is wary,—
And make a sport of it . . . They fling down pebbles,
Following, with eyes undizzied, the long curve,
The long slow outward curve, into the abyss,
As far as eye can follow; and they themselves
Turn back, unworried, to the here and now . . .
But you have been there, too?—

                                        —I saw at length
The space-defying pine, that on the last
Outjutting rock has cramped its powerful roots.
There stood I too: under that tree I stood:
My hand against its resinous bark: my face
Turned out and downward to the fourfold kingdom.
The wind roared from all quarters. The waterfall
Came down, it seemed, from Heaven. The mighty sound
Of pouring elements,—earth, air, and water,—
The cry of eagles, chatter of falling stones,—
These were the frightful language of that place.
I understood it ill, but understood.—

—You understood it? Tell me, then, its meaning.
It was an all, a nothing, or a something?
Chaos, or divine love, or emptiness?
Water and earth and air and the sun's fire?
Or else, a question, simply?—

                                  —Water and fire were there,
And air and earth; there too was emptiness;
All, and nothing, and something too, and love.
But these poor words, these squeaks of ours, in which
We strive to mimic, with strained throats and tongues,
The spawning and outrageous elements—
Alas, how paltry are they! For I saw—

—What did you see?

                              —I saw myself and God.
I saw the ruin in which godhead lives:
Shapeless and vast: the strewn wreck of the world:
Sadness unplumbed: misery without bound.
Wailing I heard, but also I heard joy.
Wreckage I saw, but also I saw flowers.
Hatred I saw, but also I saw love . . .
And thus, I saw myself.

                        —And this alone?

—And this alone awaits you, when you dare
To that sheer verge where horror hangs, and tremble
Against the falling rock; and, looking down,
Search the dark kingdom. It is to self you come,—
And that is God. It is the seed of seeds:
Seed for disastrous and immortal worlds.

It is the answer that no question asked.

XVII

And thus Narcissus, cunning with a hand-glass,
Preening a curl, and smirking, had his say.
God's pity on us all! he cried (half laughing)
That we must die: that Lesbia's curl be lost,
And Shakspere's wit forgotten; and the potter—
Who saw, one instant, all humanity,
And phrased its passion in a single figure—
That he be sunk in clay, and dumb as clay.

God's pity on us all! he cried, and turned
The guileful mirror in a guileful light;
Smiled at the fair-curved cheek, the golden hair;
The lip, the nostril, the broad brow, the hand;
Smiled at the young bright smile . . . Alas, alas,
To think that so great beauty should be lost!
This gold, and scarlet, and flushed ivory,
Be made a sport for worms!

                  But then a wonder
Deepened his gazing eyes, darkened the pupils,
Shaded his face, as if a cloud had passed.
The mirror spoke the truth. A shape he saw
Unknown before,—obscene, disastrous, huge,—
Huge as the world, and formless . . . Was this he?
This dumb, tumultuous, all-including horror?
This Caliban of rocks? this steaming pit
Of foisting hells,—circle on darker circle,—
With worlds in rings to right and left, and other
Starbearing hells within them, other heavens
Arched over chaos? . . .

He pondered the vast vision:
Saw the mad order, the inhuman god;
And his poor pity, with the mirror dropped,
Wore a new face: such brightness and such darkness,
Pitiless, as a moonblanched desert wears.

XIX

Watch long enough, and you will see the leaf
Fall from the bough. Without a sound it falls:
And soundless meets the grass . . . And so you have
A bare bough, and a dead leaf in dead grass.
Something has come and gone. And that is all.

But what were all the tumults in this action?
What wars of atoms in the twig, what ruins,
Fiery and disastrous, in the leaf?
Timeless the tumult was, but gave no sign.
Only, the leaf fell, and the bough is bare.

This is the world: there is no more than this.
The unseen and disastrous prelude, shaking
The trivial act from the terrific action.
Speak: and the ghosts of change, past and to come,
Throng the brief word. The maelstrom has us all.

XX

So, in the evening, to the simple cloister:
This place of boughs, where sounds of water, softly,
Lap on the stones. And this is what you are:
Here, in this dusty room, to which you climb
By four steep flights of stairs. The door is closed:
The furies of the city howl behind you:
The last bell plunges rock-like to the sea:
The horns of taxis wail in vain. You come
Once more, at evening, to this simple cloister;
Hushed by the quiet walls, you stand at peace.

What ferns of thought are these, the cool and green,
Dripping with moisture, that festoon these walls?
What water-lights are these, whose pallid rings
Dance with the leaves, or speckle the pale stones?
What spring is this, that bubbles the cold sand,
Urging the sluggish grains of white and gold? . . .
Peace. The delicious silence throngs with ghosts
Of wingèd sound and shadow. These are you.

Now in the evening, in the simple cloister,
You stand and wait; you stand and listen, waiting
For wingèd sounds and wingèd silences,
And long-remembered shadows. Here the rock
Lets down its vine of many colored flowers;
Waiting for you, or waiting for the lizard
To move his lifted claw, or shift his eye
Quick as a jewel. Here the lizard waits
For the slow snake to slide among cold leaves.
And, on the bough that arches the deep pool,
Lapped in a sound of water, the brown thrush
Waits, too, and listens, till his silence makes
Silence as deep as song. And time becomes
A timeless crystal, an eternity,
In which the gone and coming are at peace.

What bird is this, whose silence fills the trees
With rich delight? What leaves and boughs are these,
What lizard, and what snake? . . . The bird is gone:
And while you wait, another comes and goes,—
Another and another; yet your eye,
Although it has not moved, can scarcely say
If birds have come and gone,—so quick, so brief,—
Or if the thrush who waits there is the same . . .
The snake and lizard change, yet are the same:
The flowers, many-colored, on the vine,
Open and close their multitude of stars,—
Yet are the same . . . And all these things are you.

Thus in the evening, in the simple cloister,
Eternity adds ring to ring, the darker

Beyond the brighter; and your silence fills
With such a world of worlds,—so still, so deep,—
As never voice could speak, whether it were
The ocean's or the bird's. The night comes on:
You wait and listen, in the darkened room,
To all these ghosts of change. And they are you.

XXIX

What shall we do—what shall we think—what shall we say—?
Why, as the crocus does, on a March morning,
With just such shape and brightness; such fragility;
Such white and gold, and out of just such earth.
Or as the cloud does on the northeast wind—
Fluent and formless; or as the tree that withers.
What are we made of, strumpet, but of these?
Nothing. We are the sum of all these accidents—
Compounded all our days of idiot trifles,—
The this, the that, the other, and the next;
What x or y said, or old uncle thought;
Whether it rained or not, and at what hour;
Whether the pudding had two eggs or three,
And those we loved were ladies . . . Were they ladies?
And did they read the proper books, and simper
With proper persons, at the proper teas?
O Christ and God and all deciduous things—
Let us void out this nonsense and be healed.

There is no doubt that we shall do, as always,
Just what the crocus does. There is no doubt
Your Helen of Troy is all that she has seen,—
All filth, all beauty, all honor and deceit.
The spider's web will hang in her bright mind,—
The dead fly die there doubly; and the rat
Find sewers to his liking. She will walk
In such a world as this alone could give—
This of the moment, this mad world of mirrors
And of corrosive memory. She will know
The lecheries of the cockroach and the worm,
The chemistry of the sunset, the foul seeds

Laid by the intellect in the simple heart . . .
And knowing all these things, she will be she.

She will be also the sunrise on the grassblade—
But pay no heed to that. She will be also
The infinite tenderness of the voice of morning—
But pay no heed to that. She will be also
The grain of elmwood, and the ply of water,
Whirlings in sand and smoke, wind in the ferns,
The fixed bright eyes of dolls . . . And this is all.

XXXI

Where is that noble mind that knows no evil,
Gay insubordinations of the worm?
Discords of mishap, rash disharmonies
Sprung from disorders in the spirit's state?
If there is such, we'll have him out in public,
And have his heart out too. There is no good,
No sweet, no noble, no divine, no right,
But it is bred of rich economy
Amongst the hothead factions of the soul.
Show me that virtuous and intolerable woman
Who swears, and doubly swears, that she is good.
And feeds her virtue on a daily lie;
That simple soul who wears simplicity
As if it were a god's cloak dropped from heaven;
Who has no secrets, no, not one, and minces
Sunrise to sunset with a sunlit smile,
Her little brain and little heart wide open;
By god, we'll rip such foulness from that angel
As never charnel knew!

But if we find
In some rank purlieu of our rotting world
That stinking wretch whose rot is worse than worst:
That natural marsh of nature, in which evil
Is light as hawk to wing, and with such grace:
Him whom the noble scorn, whose eye is dark,
Who wears proud rags around a Hinnom heart:

Why, in that heart will come such power as never
Visits the virtuous, and such sweetness too
As god reserves for chaos.

XXXIII

Then came I to the shoreless shore of silence,
Where never summer was nor shade of tree,
Nor sound of water, nor sweet light of sun,
But only nothing and the shore of nothing,
Above, below, around, and in my heart:

Where day was not, not night, nor space, nor time,
Where no bird sang, save him of memory,
Nor footstep marked upon the marl, to guide
My halting footstep; and I turned for terror,
Seeking in vain the Pole Star of my thought;

Where it was blown among the shapeless clouds,
And gone as soon as seen, and scarce recalled,
Its image lost and I directionless;
Alone upon the brown sad edge of chaos,
In the wan evening that was evening always;

Then closed my eyes upon the sea of nothing
While memory brought back a sea more bright,
With long, long waves of light, and the swift sun,
And the good trees that bowed upon the wind;
And stood until grown dizzy with that dream;

Seeking in all that joy of things remembered
One image, one the dearest, one most bright,
One face, one star, one daisy, one delight,
One hour with wings most heavenly and swift,
One hand the tenderest upon my heart;

But still no image came, save of that sea,
No tenderer thing than thought of tenderness,
No heart or daisy brighter than the rest;
And only sadness at the bright sea lost,
And mournfulness that all had not been praised.

O lords of chaos, atoms of desire,
Whirlwind of fruitfulness, destruction's seed,
Hear now upon the void my late delight,
The quick brief cry of memory, that knows
At the dark's edge how great the darkness is.

XXXV

This was the gentlest creature that we knew,
This lamia of men, this sensitive
Sad soul, so poisoned, and so poisoning.
God take his bowels out, and break his bones,
And show him in the market as he is:
An angel with a peacock's heart, a fraud
With such a gilding on him as is gold.

This was the nimblest of the necromancers,
This lodestar of the mind, this tentative
Quick thought, so injured, and so injuring.
God take his conscience out, and set him free,
And break his mind to rapture, and delight
Those that would murder him, and those that love,
And those that love mankind.

XXXVII

Come let us take another's words and change the meaning,
Come let us take another's meaning, change the words,
Rebuild the house that Adam built, with opals,
Redecorate Eve's bedroom. We were born
With words, but they were not our words, but others',
Smacked of the kitchen, or of gods, or devils,
Worn and stained with the blood of centuries,
The sweat of peasants, the raw gold of kings.
Shall we be slaves to such inheritance?
No; let us sweep these skeleton leaves away,
Blow them beyond the moon; and from our anger,
Our pride, our bitterness, our sweetness too,
And what our kidneys say, and what our hearts,
Speak with such voice as never Babel heard;
And bring the curtain down on desolation.

Was this rich tongue of ours shaped by our mothers?
Has it no virtue of its own? says nothing
Not said before at church or between sheets?
Must Shakspere, with his phrase for the stormed heaven,
Hot midnight veined with lightning, babble only
Such mother's milk as one time wet his cheek?
Then let's be dumb: Walk in the little garden:
Watch the wise thrust delight as once in Egypt;
And hear the echoes of Thermopylæ.

And this is peace; to know our knowledge known;
To know ourselves but as old stones that sleep
In God's midstream of wreckage, worn as smooth.
All's commonplace: the jewel with the rest.
The demon truth, sharp as a maggot, works
His destined passage through the Absolute.

XXXVIII

When you come back from Memnon, when you come
Into the shadow, the green land of evening,
And hear the leaves above you, and the water
Falling, falling, in fountains;
When you remember Memnon, and the sand,
The stone lips crying to the desert, the stone eyes
Red with the daybreak not yet seen by you;

When you shake out the desert from your shoes
And laugh amongst you, and are refreshed,
And go about your business, now secure
Against the mockery of the all-changing moon;
And most of all, oh sly ones, when you sell
So dearly to the poor your grains of wisdom,
Or barter to the ignorant your belief;

Oh think of this belief and think it evil,
Evil for you because you heard it only
From a stone god whose prophecies you mocked;
Evil for them because their hunger buys it;
Evil for both of you, poor pitiful slaves,

Who had no heart, when chaos came again,
Who had no love, to make the chaos bright.

Go back again, and find the divine dark;
Seal up your eyes once more, and be as tombs;
See that yourselves shall be as Memnon was.
Then, if you have the strength to curse the darkness,
And praise a world of light, remember Memnon—
Stone feet in sand, stone eyes, stone heart, stone lips,
Who sang the day before the daybreak came.

XLI

Or daylong watched, in the kaleidoscope,
While the rain beat the window, and the smoke
Blew down along the roof, how the clear fragments
Clicked subtly inward to new patterns, seeming
To melt from rose to crystal, moon to star,
Snowflake to asphodel, the bright white shrinking
To let the ruby vein its way like blood,
The violet opening like an eye, the pearl
Gone like a raindrop. Never twice the same,
Never remembered. The carpet there, the table
On which the dog's-eared Euclid with fixed stars,
The cardboard battleship, the tops, the jackstones,
And the long window lustred with changing rain,
And the long day, profound and termless.

                                        Or
The ship's deck, midnight, winter, and the stars
Swung in a long curve starboard above the mast,
And bow-ward then as the sea hoists the bow,
And back to port, in a vast dance of atoms,
Poured down like snow about you, or again
Steady above the mast-light, the wide span
Of brilliant worlds, not meaningless, watched bravely
By him who guards the lighted binnacle, and him
Dark in the swaying crow's nest, who beats his arms
Against the cold. What mind of stars is this?
What changing thought that takes its ever-changing

Pattern in burning worlds, worlds dying, named
Sirius or Vega or the Pleiades?
What voyage this beneath them, termless, but
Not aimless wholly, trackless in the trackless
Changing of thought in that wide mind of stars?

Back from the bitter voyage to this moment:
Where the clock's tick marks hunger from disgust,
And the hour strikes for laughter, causeless, caused
By one strayed particle, unseen, between
The heart's Nile and the brain's unknown Sahara:
Rolando's fissure and the Island of Reil.
Who watches here, oh mariners and surgeons?
What Pole Star lights these shores? The atom grows,
If so it will, much like a tree, its light
Orion's now, and now the Bear's, the clock
Seeking in vain its time. We will go on,
Since go we must, bending our eyes above
The little space of light we know, watching
Thought come from news, love come from thought, desire
Come to fulfilment or defeat; and all
Swinging beneath us like that mind of stars,
Which alters when it must, alters for nothing,
In the long night that guides the ship to death.

XLIII

Not with despair, nor with rash hardihood,
And yet with both, salute the grassblade, take
The terrible thistledown between your hands, assume
Divinity, and ride the cloud. Come boldly
Upon the rock and count his scars, number
The ants that raid the pear, and be yourself
The multitude you are. We are destroyed
Daily. We meet the arrows of the sun,
Corruption, ruin, decay, time in the seed,
Usury in the flesh, death in the heart.
This band of sunlight on the frost—mistrust it.
This frost that measures blades against the sun—

Mistrust it. Look with meanest scrutiny on
This little clock, your slave. You, yourself—
Put up your plumes and crow, you are a clock
Unique, absolved, ridiculous, profound,
The clock that knows, if but it will, its tick
To be a tick, and nothing but a tick.
Walk them among the shadows with your measure
Of long and short and good and evil, mark
The come and go that leaves you—as you think—
Much as you were, or as you thought you were;
And when the spring breaks, stop.

                    Divine time-heart
That beats the violet to fragrance, turns
The planet westward to his fruitful death,
Gives the young sun his season, or compels
The hand to seek the cheek—

                    I saw the evening
Giving her daily bread, and heard the prayers
Of proud weeds answered, saw the ritual
With which indifferent moss and tree were married,
The steeples pointed to the absolute,
Man avoided man, star avoided star,
The rocks were single in hard humbleness;
And thought alone it was that in its weakness
Sought answering thought.

                  Divine time-thought
That brings the dead man home to underground,
Blessing the resurrection for no reason;
Giving the child his candlelight of love,
Briefly and snatched away, that he be wise—
And know in time, the dark—

                  I saw the morning
Promise his daily bread, heard the Lord's Prayer
Whispered by sea-grass for the Lord himself:
That thought be thought no more, that heart be heart
Henceforward, timeless; and I was deceived,

133

Wishing to be deceived; and wise in this;
And touched a rock, and became rock forever.

XLIV

When you have done your murder, and the word
Lies bleeding, and the hangman's noose
Coils like a snake and hisses against your neck—
When the beloved, the adored, the word
Brought from the sunrise at the rainbow's foot
Lies dead, the first of all things now the last—

Rejoice, gay fool, laugh at the pit's edge, now
Heaven is come again, you are yourself
As once you were, the sunrise word has gone
Into the heart again, all's well with you,
Now for an instant's rapture you are only
The sunrise word, naught else, and you have wings
Lost from your second day.

                  Wisdom of wings,
Angelic power, divinity, destruction
Perfect in itself—the sword is heartshaped,
The word is bloodshaped, the flower is a coffin,
The world is everlasting—

                  But for a moment only,
The sunrise sunset moment at the pit's edge,
The night in day, timeless for a time:
Childhood is old age, youth is maturity,
Simplicity is power, the single heart
Cries like Memnon for the sun, his giant hand
Lifting the sun from the eastern hill, and then
Handing it to the west—

                And in that moment
All known, all good, all beautiful; the child
Ruling his god, as god intends he should.

XLV

The dead man spoke to me and begged a penny,
For god's sake, and for yours and mine, he said,
Slowly under the streetlamp turned his head,
I saw his eyes wide open and he stared
Through me as if my bones and flesh were nothing,
Through me and through the earth and through the void,
His eyes were dark and wide and cold and empty
As if his vision had become a grave
Larger than bones of any world could fill,
But crystal clear and deep and deeply still.

Poor devil—why, he wants to close his eyes,
He wants a charity to close his eyes,
And follows me with outstretched palm, from world to world
And house to house and street to street,
Under the streetlamps and along dark alleys,
And sits beside me in my room, and sleeps
Upright with eyes wide open by my bed,
Circles the Pleiades with a glance, returns
From cold Orion with a slow turn of the head,
Looks north and south at once, and all the while
Holds, in that void of an unfocussed stare,
My own poor footsteps, saying

                              I have read
Time in the rock and in the human heart,
Space in the bloodstream, and those lesser works
Written by rose and windflower on the summer, sung
By water and snow, deciphered by the eye,
Translated by the slaves of memory,
And all that you be you, and I be I,
Or all that by imagination, aping
God, the supreme poet of despair,
I may be you, you me, before our time
Knowing the rank intolerable taste of death,
And walking dead on the still living earth.

. . . I rose and dressed and descended the stair
Into the sunlight, and he came with me,
Staring the skeleton from the daffodil,
Freezing the snowflake in the blackbird's whistle,
And with that cold profound unhating eye
He moved the universe from east to west,
Slowly, disastrously,—but with such splendor
As god, the supreme poet of delight, might envy,—
To the magnificent sepulchre of sleep.

XLVIII

Pawn to king four; pawn to king four; pawn
To king's knight four—the gambit is declined.
The obvious is declined; and we adventure
For stranger mishap than would here have fallen.
Where would the victory have led us, what
New square might thus have witnessed our defeat?
The king is murdered in his counting-house;
Or at the table, where he carves a fowl;
Stabbed by his light-of-love; drowned in his bath;
And all that he might know—

                              Why, something new;
Such sport of nature as deforms a leaf
Or gives the toad a wing. Thus we find
The afternoon, for all its honeyed light
On gilded lawns, is monstrous grown, profound
Induction to such hell as Blake himself
Had never guessed. Suddenly comes the Queen
Dressed like a playing-card; a wind of fear
Flutters the courtiers; and the garden strewn
With the blown wreckage of our flimsy world.
And the poor king, bewildered, stops his heart
On the loud note of doubt.

                              Yet, let us risk
This tame avoidance of the obvious.
Inward or outward, let the maze invite

The poor mind, avid of complexities,
And wrap it in confusion. It is here,
When tearing web from web, that we most answer
The insistent question of the will-to-be;
The eternal challenge of the absolute;
And it is here

                    most brightly comes false nature in a mask,
The mincing queen of loveliness, and smiles
Witchery, through her painted smile of hate.
Shall we succumb? or through the garden gate
Make such an exit as no trumpets sound?
Shall we be mannered, and let manners lead us
Through nimble mockery and dance of wits
Which we know well that only death will end?
O take her hand, poor king, make love to her;
Praise her false beauty, which is richly true;
Walk in the coverts with her, kiss that mask
Whose poison kills the subject it inflames;
And when you feel the venom chill your blood,
Then look about you, then with leisure smile
At all denied you and at all you know;
Count the bright minutes; pick a flower and smell it;
Observe the lights and shadows; theorize
Magnificently of life and death: propound
The subtle thesis of pure consciousness . . .
And bow, and leave the world one wit the less.

L

The world is intricate, and we are nothing.
The world is nothing: we are intricate.
Alas, how simple to invert the world
Inverting phrases! And, alas, how simple
To fool the foolish heart to his topmost bent
With flattery of the moment! Add, subtract,
Divide or subdivide with verbs and adverbs,
Multiply adjectives like cockatoos
That scream lewd colors in a phrase of trees;

Or else, with watery parentheses,
Dilute the current of your pain, divert
The red Nile's anguish till at last it waste
In sleepy deltas of slow anodyne:
Turn, with a word, the hæmorrhage to a glacier;
And all that—fools!—we may enjoy (this moment).
Precisely what we are.

                  Despair, delight,
That we should be thus trapped in our own minds!
O this ambiguous nature in the blood
That wills and wills not, thinks and thinks not, hates
What it most loves, destroys what it desires,
Dissects, with skeleton's algebra, the heart!
Which will we keep? the heart? the algebra?
Will Euclid guide us safely to our tombs?
Must we renew man's venture round the Poles—
Seek, through the brain, some colder Northwest Passage—
Reason our way by inches to the frost
And frozen die in triumph? This were death
Noble indeed, enjoined of god, for those
Who think it noble and enjoined of god.
Thus let us perish. We have been round the Cape
With Freud, the sea-gull, Einstein, and the Bear;
Lived on the sea-moss of the absolute;
And died in wisdom, and been glad to die.

But let us die as gladly for such reasons
As have no reason: let us die as fools,
If so we will; explore the rash heart's folly;
The marshes of the Congo of the blood.
Here are such wisdoms—who knows?—as pure wisdom
Knows nothing of. Such birds of Paradise,—
Delusory,—as Euclid never knew,—
Colors of our own madness, and of god's . . .
O humans! Let us venture still, and die,
Alternately, of madness and of truth.

LII

Stood, at the closed door, and remembered—
Hand on the doorpost faltered, and remembered—
The long ago, the far away, the near
With its absurdities—the calendar,
The one-eyed calendar upon the wall,
And time dispersed, and in a thousand ways,
Calendars torn, appointments made and kept,
Or made and broken, and the shoes worn out
Going and coming, street and stair and street,
Lamplight and starlight, fog and northeast wind,
St. Mary's ringing the angelus at six—

And it was there, at eight o'clock, I saw
Vivien and the infinite, together,
And it was here I signed my name in pencil
Against the doorpost, and later saw the snow
Left by the messenger, and here were voices—
Come back later, do come back later, if you can,
And tell us what it was, tell us what you saw,
Put your heart on the table with your hand
And tell us all those secrets that are known
In the profound interstices of time—
The glee, the wickedness, the smirk, the sudden
Divine delight—do come back and tell us,
The clock has stopped, sunset is on the snow,
Midnight is far away, and morning farther—

And then the trains that cried at night, the ships
That mourned in fog, the days whose gift was rain,
June's daisy, and she loved me not, the skull
Brought from the tomb—and I was there, and saw
The bright spade break the bone, the trumpet-vine
Bugled with bees, and on my knees I picked
One small white clover in the cactus shade,
Put it in water and took it to that room
Where blinds were drawn and all was still—

Neighbors, I have come
From a vast everything whose sum is nothing,
From a complexity whose speech is simple,
Here are my hands and heart, and I have brought
Nothing you do not know, and do not fear.
Here is the evening paper at your door—
Here are your letters, I have brought the tickets,
The hour is early, and the speech is late.
Come, we are gods,—let us discourse as gods;
And weigh the grain of sand with Socrates;
Before we fall to kissing, and to bed.

LIII

Nothing to say, you say? Then we'll say nothing:
But step from rug to rug and hold our breaths,
Count the green ivy-strings against the window,
The pictures on the wall. Let us exchange
Pennies of gossip, news from nowhere, names
Held in despite or honor; we have seen
The weather-vanes veer westward, and the clouds
Obedient to the wind; have walked in snow;
Forgotten and remembered—

                  But we are strangers;
Came here by paths which never crossed; and stare
At the blind mystery of each to each.
You've seen the sea and mountains? taken ether?
And slept in hospitals from Rome to Cairo?
Why so have I; and lost my tonsils, too;
And drunk the waters of the absolute.
But is it this we meet for, of an evening,
Is it this—

        O come, like Shelley,
For god's sake let us sit on honest ground
And tell harsh stories of the deaths of kings!
Have out our hearts, confess our blood,
Our foulness and our virtue! I have known
Such sunsets of despair as god himself

Might weep for of a Sunday; and then slept
As dreamlessly as Jesus in his tomb.
I have had time in one hand, space in the other,
And mixed them to no purpose. I have seen
More in a woman's eye than can be liked,
And less than can be known. And as for you—

O creature of the frost and sunlight, worm
Uplifted by the atom's joy, receiver
Of stolen goods, unconscious thief of god—
Tell me upon this sofa how you came
From darkness to this darkness, from what terroi
You found this restless pause in terror, learned
The bitter light you follow. We will talk—

But it is time to go, and I must go;
And what we thought, and silenced, none shall know

LVI

Rimbaud and Verlaine, precious pair of poets,
Genius in both (but what is genius?) playing
Chess on a marble table at an inn
With chestnut blossom falling in blond beer
And on their hair and between knight and bishop—
Sunlight squared between them on the chess-board
Cirrus in heaven, and a squeal of music
Blown from the leathern door of Ste. Sulpice—

Discussing, between moves, iamb and spondee
Anacoluthon and the open vowel
God the great peacock with his angel peacocks
And his dependent peacocks the bright stars:
Disputing too of fate as Plato loved it,
Or Sophocles, who hated and admired,
Oi Socrates, who loved and was amused:

Verlaine puts down his pawn upon a leaf
And closes his long eyes, which are dishonest,
And says 'Rimbaud, there is one thing to do:

We must take rhetoric, and wring its neck! . . .'
Rimbaud considers gravely, moves his Queen;
And then removes himself to Timbuctoo.

And Verlaine dead,—with all his jades and mauves;
And Rimbaud dead in Marseilles with a vision,
His leg cut off, as once before his heart;
And all reported by a later lackey,
Whose virtue is his tardiness in time.

Let us describe the evening as it is:—
The stars disposed in heaven as they are:
Verlaine and Shakspere rotting, where they rot,
Rimbaud remembered, and too soon forgot;

Order in all things, logic in the dark;
Arrangement in the atom and the spark;
Time in the heart and sequence in the brain—

Such as destroyed Rimbaud and fooled Verlaine.
And let us then take godhead by the neck—

And strangle it, and with it, rhetoric.

LXII

I read the primrose and the sea
                    and remember nothing
I read Arcturus and the snow
                    and remember nothing
I read the green and white book of spring
                    and remember nothing
I read the hatred in a man's eye
                    Lord, I remember nothing.

Scorn spat at me and spoke
                    I remember it not
The river was frozen round the ship
                    I remember it not

I found a secret message in a blade of grass
                    and it is forgotten
I called my lovers by their sweet names
                    they are all forgotten.

Where are my lovers now?
                    buried in me.
The blades of grass, the ships, the scorners?
                    here in me
The haters in the spring, snow and Arcturus?
                    here in me
The primrose and the sea?
                    here in me.

I know what humans know
                    no less no more
I know how the summer breaks
                    on Neptune's shore
I know how winter freezes
                    the Milky Way
My heart's home is in Limbo
                    and there I stay.

Praise Limbo, heart, and praise
                    forgetfulness
We know what the tiger knows
                    no more no less
We know what the primrose thinks
                    and think it too
We walk when the snail walks
                    across the dew.

I was a rash man in my time
                    but now I am still
I spoke with god's voice once
                    now I am still
Evil made my right hand strong
                    which now is still
Wisdom gave me pride once,
                    but it is still.

Lie down poor heart at last
                        and have your rest
Remember to forget
                        and have your rest
Think of yourself as once you were
                        at your best
And then lie down alone
                        and have your rest.

These things are as time weaves them
                        on his loom
Forgot, forgetting, we survive not
                        mortal bloom
Let us give thanks, to space,
                        for a little room
Space is our face and time our death
                        two poles of doom

Come dance around the compass
                        pointing north
Before, face downward, frozen,
                        we go forth.

LXIII

Thus systole addressed diastole,—
The heart contracting, with its grief of burden,
To the lax heart, with grief of burden gone.

Thus star to dead leaf speaks; thus cliff to sea;
And thus the spider, on a summer's day,
To the bright thistledown, trapped in the web.

No language leaps this chasm like a lightning:
Here is no message of assuagement, blown
From Ecuador to Greenland; here is only

A trumpet blast, that calls dead men to arms;
The granite's pity for the cloud; the whisper
Of time to space.

Time in the Rock
OR
PRELUDES TO DEFINITION

I

And there I saw the seed upon the mountain
but it was not a seed it was a star
but it was not a star it was a world
but it was not a world it was a god
but it as not a god it was a laughter

blood red within and lightning for its rind
the root came out like gold and it was anger
the root came out like fire and it was fury
the root came out like horn and it was purpose
but it was not a root it was a hand

destructive strong and eager full of blood
and broke the rocks and set them on each other
and broke the waters into shafts of light
and set them end to end and made them seas
and out of laughter wrung a grief of water

and thus beneath the web of mind I saw
under the west and east of web I saw
under the bloodshot spawn of stars I saw
under the water and the inarticulate laughter
the coiling down the coiling in the coiling

mean and intense and furious and secret
profound and evil and despatched in darkness
shot homeward foully in a filth of effort
clotted and quick and thick and without aim
spasm of concentration of the sea

and there I saw the seed upon the shore
but it was not a seed it was a man
but it was not a man it was a god
magnificent and humble in the morning
with angels poised upon his either hand.

II

We need a theme? then let that be our theme:
that we, poor grovellers between faith and doubt,
the sun and north star lost, and compass out,
the heart's weak engine all but stopped, the time
timeless in this chaos of our wills—
that we must ask a theme, something to think,
something to say, between dawn and dark,
something to hold to, something to love—

Medusa of the northern sky, shine upon us,
and if we fear to think, then turn that fear to stone,
that we may learn unconsciousness alone;
but freeze not the uplifted prayer of hands
that hope for the unknown.

Give us this day our daily death, that we
may learn to live;
teach us that we trespass; that we may learn,
in wisdom, not in kindness, to forgive;
and in the granite of our own bones seal us daily.

O neighbors, in this world of dooms and omens,
participators in the crime of god,
seekers of self amid the ruins of space:
jurors and guilty men, who, face to face,
discover you but judge yourselves to death,
and for such guilt as god himself prepared,—
dreamed in the atom, and so brought to birth
between one zero and another,—

                              turn again
to the cold violet that braves the snow,

the murder in the tiger's eye, the pure
indifference in the star. Why, we are come
at last to that bright verge where god himself
dares for the first time, with unfaltering foot.
And can we falter, who ourselves are god?

III

Envy is holy. Let us envy those
bright angels whose bright wings are stronger far
than the bare arms we lift toward the star.
And hate them too; until our hate has grown
to wings more powerful than angels' wings;
when with a vaulting step, from the bare mountain,
we'll breathe the empyrean; and so wheel
gladly to earth again.

               Then we shall see
and love that humbleness which was ourselves;
it will be home to us; until such time
as our strong wings, in their own majesty,
themselves will lift us to another world;
from which is no return.

               But in that world,
there too burn higher angels, whose wide wings
outspan us, shadow us hugely, and outsoar us;
rainbows of such magnificent height
as hide the stars; and under these we'll cower
envious and hateful; and we will envy,
till once again, with contumacious wings,
ourselves will mount to a new terror, wheel
slowly once more, but gratefully, and gladly,
to home in limbo.

        And thus North forever.

V

Out of your sickness let your sickness speak—
the bile must have his way—the blood his froth—
poison will come to the tongue. Is hell your kingdom?
you know its privies and its purlieus? keep
sad record of its filth? Why this is health:
there is no other, save what angels know.

Ravel the pattern backward, to no pattern:
reduce the granite downward, to no stone:
unhinge the rainbow to his sun and rain:
dissolve the blood to water and to salt:
is this dishevelment we cannot bear?
The angel is the one who knows his wings!

You came from darkness, and you now remember
darkness, terror, windows to a world,
horror of light, cold hands in violence thrust,
tyrants diastole and systole.
O cling to warmth, poor child, and press your mouth
against the warm all-poisoning side of the world.

She's there, she's there,—whispering at all hours—
defending and deluding and defending—
she's in your heart, she's in your traitor blood,
arches your eyebrow and contracts your eye.
Alas, what help for you, poor orphan fool,
who creep from rib to rib, and lose your way?

Let poison spit its blister from your tongue:
let horror break the left side of your heart,
the brightest syllable be drowned in blood—:
thus to the knowledge of your wings you come,
O angel, man! and thus to wisdom bring
terror from terror, and the Thing from thing.

X

True inwardness—ah! there is such a phrase—?
the truth is inward, and not outward—the oak tree
false in the bark, false in leaf or mast,
true only in the root? and you, poor biped,
who rise in the morning to walk and talk—

are the shoes that await you by the chair
less true than the dreams from which you wake, the hat
that hangs in the hall less true than memory
which remembers it, reaches a hand to it,—
the door less true than the hand that shuts it?

Move outward, and you only move, poor biped,
an atom's atom from here to here, never
from here to there—again your 'self' you meet,
it is yourself that waits outside the door,
salutes you on the waking side of dream—

hands you your coat, your collar, the new necktie,
directs your appetite, chooses an egg,
says, as you read the morning paper, act
or do not act, reflect, do not reflect,
love viciously, love wisely, love not at all—

this is 'you,' this headline in the news,
the news is 'you,' is old already, undiscovered
is 'you,' too, long discovered. Greet your face—
dispersed in some such terms, phrased, rephrased;
speak to that farthest star, which is yourself!

Are these less 'you' than the decayed molar?
the lost appendix? the leaky heart? the mind
too much delayed by daily bread of sex?
Learn the truth outwardness of inner truth!
time will at last bring both at once to end.

For at one stroke—no matter whence it come—
lightning or ice or blood—inward and outward
will singularly cease, and be the same.
Then history will give to both a name;
and so at last those things so bravely done
will be at peace with what was merely known.

XI

Mysticism, but let us have no words,
angels, but let us have no fantasies,
churches, but let us have no creeds,
no dead gods hung on crosses in a shop,
nor beads nor prayers nor faith nor sin nor penance:
and yet, let us believe, let us believe.

Let it be the flower
seen by the child for the first time, plucked without thought
broken for love and as soon forgotten:

and the angels, let them be our friends,
used for our needs with selfish simplicity,
broken for love and as soon forgotten;

and let the churches be our houses
defiled daily, loud with discord,—
where the dead gods that were our selves may hang,
our outgrown gods on every wall;
Christ on the mantelpiece, with downcast eyes;
Buddha above the stove;
the Holy Ghost by the hatrack, and God himself
staring like Narcissus from the mirror,
clad in a raincoat, and with hat and gloves.

Mysticism, but let it be a flower,
let it be the hand that reaches for the flower,
let it be the flower that imagined the first hand,
let it be the space that removed itself to give place
for the hand that reaches, the flower to be reached—

let it be self displacing self
as quietly as a child lifts a pebble,
as softly as a flower decides to fall,—
self replacing self
as seed follows flower to earth.

XII

One cricket said to another—
come, let us be ridiculous, and say love!
love love love love love
let us be absurd, woman, and say hate!
hate hate hate hate hate
and then let us be angelic and say nothing.

And the other cricket said to the first—
fool! fool! speak! speak! speak!
speak if you must, but speaking speaking speaking
what docs it gct us, what docs it gct us, what?
act act act act give
giving is love, giving is love, give!

One cricket said to another—
what is love what is love what is love
act—speak—act—spcak—act—spcak—
give—take—give—take—give—take—
more slowly as the autumn comes, but giving
and taking still,—you taking, and I giving!

And the other cricket said to the first—
yes! yes! yes! you give your word!
words words but what at the end are words
speech speech what is the use of speech
give me love give me love
love!

One cricket said to another—
in the beginning—I forget—in the beginning—
fool fool fool fool fool

too late to remember and too late to teach—
in the beginning was the word, the speech,
and in the end the word, the word, the word . . .

But while they quarrelled, these two foolish crickets,
and bandied act with word, denying each,
weighing their actions out in terms of speech,
the frost came whitely down and furred them both,
the speech grew slower, and the action nil,
and, at the end, even the word was still;
and god began again.

XIII

As if god were a gypsy in a tent,
the smeared mask in the smoky light,
smiling with concealed intent—
pointing to the bag of fortunes from which you choose—
his hand like a claw, a tiger's claw,
the claw with stripes—

            (as if one thus, in the twilight,
at the hour of the bat, the hour of the moth,
when night-eyes open and day-eyes close,
saw, in the flitting betwixt light and light,
the half-knowledge which is more than knowledge,—)

saying choose now—the time is come—put in your hand—
take out the card that tells your future—
five words or six in vast calligraphy
spaced paused and pointed as they should be, printed
in words of Alpha, in words of Omega
or in such words as are not words at all—
thunder, harsh lightning, the fierce asterisk
that stars the word for footnote to dead worlds—
choose now, be doomed, take out the phrase
that calls you king, that calls you fool,
brings the fat klondyke to too greedy hands—

as if you saw

the crass inevitable and stupid finger
thrust then among the alien cards, alien phrases,
your finger, injured by life, already willing
to turn one way, rather than another—

and saw it choose

one phrase, one idiot round of idiot words
(how can you say your scorn for this deception)
one phrase, one sullen phrase, to be the symbol
of all you are—to be the ambassador
of all you are to all that is not you—

if life were this, if soul were only this,
as well it might be, should be, must be, is—
god the proud gypsy in his tent at twilight
yourself the fool that darkling takes a card—:
your life thus blindfold dedicate to folly,
murder become a hand, hand become murder
by patient evolution—

Think of this,

and laugh, at moth's hour, bat's hour, or at wolf's hour,—
that moth be moth, bat be bat, wolf be wolf,—
that gypsy be a god;
shuffler of cards, and cozener of fools.

XVI

Went home so, laughing, the foolish one, who knew
(or thought he knew, and thinking is to know)
the bitter, brief, and bright, the morning's madness,
the evening's folly. So took home with him
a card, a glove, a letter, and the word
spoken and laughed at and denied, the word
born in the heart, but stillborn: the denial
of grassblade's heart.

Has the grassblade a heart?

morning a pulse? the human hand a meaning?
was there a purpose in my name this morning?

153

This is a day of dreadful commonplace;
of news and newspapers and date and action;
I brushed my teeth, and drank my coffee, saw
sunlight among the dishes, spoke the word
that breakfast dictates; saw the immortal worm
under the table and beneath the world,
working his comic passage toward death.

How there, old fellow, and have you come again,
you that I saw beneath my fingernail,
who ate my sweetheart's eyelid and her eye—
who ruin the daylight and delight in dark,
follow me to my birth and to my death,
sit in my breath and chuckle in my heart—

must you be always where delight is brightest
let fall your seed beneath the hawthorn blossom,
scream behind rainbows? I have seen your wings.
Know you. You are that fellow who was born
under my name, but with a different meaning:

you are that fellow whose precocious death
leads me to graveyards in the glare of noon,
and murmurs murder in the bridal bed.
Lie down: we are absolved: we go from here
to wider emptiness, and such dispersals
of death, and cruelty, and the death of pain,
as no life knew before, or will know after.

XVII

Sad softness of control, unceasing censor,
multiple ghost, white Cerberus of the soul
whose melancholy baying guards the moon
above the sleeping eye—

                    must we be angry
as the tree is angry, angry with the wind,
the leaves angry, borne down or up
striving in vain for rest

                    are the roots angry
thrusting in agony against the stone
urging their grief against the dark, waiting,
and yet not waiting, for inconceivable rest

must we be angry with the wind and stone
exert the blood against the permanent horror
wind inward, downward, upward, without pause,
resist resistance, and all for nothing?

Sad softness of control, unceasing censor
what is your purpose in perpetual midnight
you who say wait, you who say pause,
whose word, whose only word is always no-yes,
the ambiguity, the evasion, the dishonesty
which is the sum of all our honesties

the sifting one, ambivalent one, the honesty
which is the sum of all dishonesties—
total of stars which is a thought of darkness
total of darkness which is a thought of stars—

must we be angry, that we at last be still
violently move that we at last find peace
be restless that we know the price of pause?
where is the sleep we came from, where the sleep—
midnight, without irritant of stars—
knowledge without memory?

                    Let us be angry
wake and be angry with the wind and stone
and know the loneliness of being alone.

XIX

This image or another, this quick choosing,
raindrop choosing a path through grains of sand
the blood-drop choosing its way, that the dead world
may wake and think or sleep and dream

This gesture or another, this quick action
the bough broken by the wind and flung down
the hand striking or touching, that the dead world
may know itself and forget itself

This memory or another, this brief picture
sunbeam on the shrivelled and frosted leaf
a world of selves trying to remember the self
before the idea of self is lost—

Walk with me world, upon my right hand walk,
speak to me Babel, that I may strive to assemble
of all these syllables a single word
before the purpose of speech is gone.

XXI

Deep violet, deep snow-cloud, deep despair,
deep root, deep pain, deep morning—must we say
deepness in all things, find our lives in deepness?
we too are deep? the breakfast salutation,
that too is deep? Alas, poor Arabel,
poor woman, poor deluded human, you
who finick with a fork and eat an egg,
are you as deep as thought of you is deep?

Timeless. The morning is not deep as thought.
Spaceless. The noon is not as deep as dream.
Formless. The night is not as deep as death.
And I defer the notion of the infinite,
the thought of you, the thought of morning,
idea of evening, idea of noon.

XXII

If man, that angel of bright consciousness,
that wingless mind and brief epitome
of god's forgetfulness, will be going forth

into the treacherous envelope of sunlight—
why, the poor fool, does he expect, does he expect
to return at evening? or to return the same?
Those who have put on, in the morning,
that cloak of light, that sheath of air,
wrapped themselves suddenly, on the exit,
in the wild wave of daybreak, which has come
from cruel Alpha,—what has become of them?
They will return as the sons of darkness.

If woman, that demon of unconsciousness,
that wingèd body of delightful chaos,
that quick embodied treason and deceit,
will go forth sinuously from the opening door
and take to herself the garment of daylight—
who will vouch for her, go her surety,
who will her bondsman be, or swear by the cloud
that she, who thus went forth, will thus come back?
If she took darkness with her, will she return
with luminous heart, and a soft light within?
For that which goes forth comes back changed or dead.

If the child, that frail mirror of the sky,
that little room of foolish laughter and grief,
transient toucher and taster of the surface,
assembler and scatterer of light,—if he go forth
into the simple street to count its stones,
its walls, its houses, its weeds and grassblades,
so, in the numbered, to sum the infinite—
infant compendium of the terrible—:
will the changed man, and the changed woman,
await him, with full knowledge, in the evening—
salute him gravely, with a kiss or handshake,
oblique embrace of the young wingless shoulders—
will they, unknowing, unknown, know this Unknown?

All three at evening, when they return once more
from the black ocean of dark Omega,
by those wild waves washed up with stars and hours,
brought home at last from nowhere to nothing—
all three will pause in the simple light,

and speak to each other, slowly, with such queer speech
as dead men use among the asphodels;
nor know each other; nor understand each other;
but tread apart on the wind, like dancers
borne by unearthly music to unearthly peace.

The house of evening, the house of clouds, vast hall
of which the walls are walls of everywhere,
enfolds them, like a wind which blows out lights.
And they are there, lying apart, lying alone,
those three who went forth suddenly in the morning
and now return, estranged and changed;
each is alone, with his extinguished lamp;
each one would weep, if he had time to weep;
but, before tears can fall, they are asleep.

XXV

The picture world, that falls apart, and leaves
a snowflake on the hand, a star of ice,
a hillside, a dead leaf

                  the picture world,
the lost and broken child's book, whence we treasure
one picture, torn and soiled, the faded colours
precious because dimmed, clear because faded,
the picture world, which is ourselves, speaking
of yesterday, and yesterday, and yesterday,
the huge world promised in the bud of May,
the leaf, the stone, the rain, the cloud,
the face most loved, the hand most clung to—

must we go back to this and have this always:
remember what was lost or what was torn:
replace the missing with a better dream
built from the broken fabric of our wills—
thus to admit our present is our past,
and in one picture find unaltered heaven—

or, shall we be angelic, close brave wings,
fall through the fathomless, feel the cold void,
and sound the darkness of the newly known?—
To face the terror in this rain that comes
across the drowned world to the drowning window;
be ignorant of rain, this unknown rain;
unknown and wild as the world was to god
when first he opened eyes—ah surely this
were nobler answer than the glib speech of habit,
the well-worn words and ready phrase, that build
comfortable walls against the wilderness?
Seeing, to know the terror of seeing: being,
to know the terror of being: knowing, to know
the dreadfulness of knowledge:

                         Come, let us drown in rain,
cry out and drown in this wild single drop,
sound the pure terror on steadfast wings, and find
in death itself the retrospective joy
held, like a picture-book, in a drowned hand.

XXVIII

And this digester, this digester of food,
this killer and eater and digester of food,
the one with teeth and tongue, insatiable belly,
him of the gut and appetite and murder,
the one with claws, the one with a quick eye,
whose footstep—ah—is soft as treason—
this foul embodied greed, this blind intestine—
this human, you or me—

                      look sharply at him
and measure him, digesters! hear his speech,
woven deceit, colossal dream, so shaped
of food and search for food—oh believe him
whose hunger shapes itself as gods and rainbows

is he not perfect, walks he not divinely
with a light step among the stars his fathers

with a quick thought among the seeds his sons
is he not graceful, is he not gentle,
this foul receiver and expeller of food,
this channel of corruption,

                              is he not
the harbinger, the angel, the bright prophet
who knows the right from wrong, whose thought is pure,
dissects the angles, numbers pains and pleasures,
dreams like an algebra among waste worlds—
can we not trust him, sees he not the sure,
disposes time and space, condemns the evil-doer—
is his digestion not an ample measure?

Come, rooted ones, come radicals, come trees,
whose powerful tentacles suck earth, and join
the murderous angels; and let us dance together
the dance of joyful cruelty, whence thrives
this world of qualities which filth ordained.

XXXVII

Where we were walking in the day's light, seeing
the flight of bones to the stars, the voyage of dead men,
those who go forth like dead leaves on the air
in the long journey, those who are swept
on the last current, the cold and shoreless ones,
who do not speak, do not answer, have no names,
nor are assembled again by any thought, but voyage
in the wide circle, the great circle

where we were talking, in the day's light, watching
even as I took your hand, even as I kissed you,
ah the unspeakable voyage of the dead men
those who go up from the grass without laughter
who take leave of the wheat and water without speech
who pass us without memory and without murmur
as they begin the endless voyage

                              where we stood
in the little round of colour, perilously poised
in the bright instant between two instant deaths,
whispering yes, whispering no, greeting and permitting,
touching and recalling, and with our eyes
looking into the past to see if there the future
might grow like a leaf, might grow like a bough with flowers,
might grow like a tree with beneficent shade

but what delight that was, O wave who broke
out of the long dark nothing against my breast,
you who lifted me violently so that we rose together,
what delight that was, in that clear instant,
even as we shone thus, the first, the last,
to see the flight of bones, the everlasting,
the noiseless unhurrying flight
of the cold and shoreless ones, the ones who no more
answer to any names, whose voyage in space
does not remember the earth or stars
nor is recalled by any spider, or any flower,
the joyless and deathless dancers—

                              speak once, speak twice,
before we join them, lady, and speak no more.

XXXVIII

Then it was that the child first spoke to me
the innocent the clear in the clear morning
the young voice finding the first sounds of joy
first sounds of grief of terror of despair
the weak hand holding mine, that was no stronger,
as if for guidance, who was my guide, though younger

so that we walked together in the cool garden
he that was innocent but knew it not
who in the thrush's song heard terror and delight
and a wide fear in the wide wave of light
joy and sorrow in the coolness of the shade
strength in my hand my hand that was afraid

myself the guilty one alas who tried to learn
new innocence by giving back my shame
into those eyes of laughter which became
guilty and frightened as I learned new joy
alas alas that thus the garden way
leads the old footstep with the young astray

he into a cloud walking I into a sun
forgive me child that thus we become one
forgive the things that teach us thus to cherish
the dread exchange by which we love and perish
forgive us trees forgive us garden path
that grief buys happiness and love buys wrath

under the thrush's voice walking back slowly
the holy innocence became unholy
the younger hand grew older and stronger
the world-stained hand grew fairer and younger
together sharing the adulterous union
which is the dreadful secret of communion

now let the murderer hide shameful eyes
behind young wings new-come from paradise
and let this angel take and hold the knife
bewildered by the murder which is life
thus in the middle noon to come together
stained hand and immaculate feather.

XXXIX

On that wild verge in the late light he stood,
the last one, who was alone, the naked one,
wingless unhappy one who had climbed there,
bruised foot and bruised hand,
first beholder of the indecipherable land,

the nameless land, the selfless land,
stood and beheld it from the granite cliff
the far beneath, the far beyond, the far above,

water and wind, the cry of the alone
his own the valley, his own the unthinking stone

and said—as I with labor have shaped this,
out of a cloud this world of rock and water,
as I have wrought with thought, or unthinking wrought,
so that a dream is brought
in agony and joy to such a realm as this

let now some god take also me and mould me
some vast and dreadful or divine dream hold me
and shape me suddenly beyond my purpose
beyond my power
to a new wilderness of hour

that I may be to him as this to me,
out of a cloud made shore and sea,
instant agony and then the splendid shape
in which is his escape,
myself at last only a well-made dream to be—

and as he spoke, his own divine dream took
sudden kingdom of the wide world, and broke
the orders into rainbows, the numbers down,
all things to nothing; and he himself became
a cloud, in which the lightning dreamed a name.

XLI

In the clear shaft of light the child so standing
alone, but his aloneness yet unknown,
all things accepting, all things at random heeding,
nearest pebble and farthest star commanding,
sorrow and joy his own
to do his bidding.

In the clear shaft of light, whether the tree
were moved by the wind or still,
alone on the flowered hill

there with the birdsong and the time song
day song and wind song
all things himself to be

So that the leaves himself became
and the green hill made answer to his name
and all things knew him who himself knew all—
so that, the sun obscured by clouds, the light
absent, he too was absent with delight,
thus went, thus came

He with the pebble in his lifted hand
whose footsteps might be traced
by flower or grass displaced—
now gone, now here, now far, now near,
now fallen in shadow beyond the rim of death
again brought homeward by lightly taken breath—

O simple one, happy one, vague one, nimble one,
has time come over your hill
has time with long bells told you, told
and do you stand there still,
among dead flowers, the sunlight gone,
your hill grown old?

In the clear shaft of light the man so standing
alone, but his aloneness known,
all things accepting, all things gladly heeding,
the heart beating, the hand bleeding,
the lost world now again his own
and marvellous with understanding.

XLII

Who would carve words must carve himself
first carve himself—

                    O carpenter,
you whose hand held nails
who knew the plane tree and the oak tree

                                              with heavy adze
hardening the muscle that became the word

and you, the sculptor, who made of hemlock wood
the little doll, or cut blind eyes in stone,
                                              habitual stroke
hammering the memory to rock precision,
god and logos, well-tempered question in the chisel,
who knew the kindness of fatigue—

                                    rising or stooping
these angels of mankind these devils of wit
sifters of habit and deceivers only
as the trained muscle deceives the mind, or feeds with custom:
these who were often tired
strengthening backs for weight of tree or stone,
or what might else of burden come from man—

who would carve words must carve himself,
first carve himself; and then alas
finds, too late, that Word is only Hand.

XLIV

Where without speech the angel walked I went
and strove as silently as he to move
seeking in his deep kindness my content
and in his grace my love

walked without word and held my arms as wings
from stone to stone as gently stepped as he
observed humility with humble things
as I himself might be:

till he it was at last who stood and spoke—
Be man, if man you be! Or be ashamed.
And turned and strode away. And on that stroke,
(as if now I were named)

in my own heart I looked, and saw the plan
for murder unadmitted. Then I knew
how mean the angel is who apes the man,
or man to man untrue

if he enact the angel. In that hour,
I did the murder I had planned; and then
sought out that fellow, my own dream of power,
and mimicked him again.

XLVII

Not with the noting of a private hate,
as if one put a mark down in a book;
nor with the chronicling of a private love,
as if one cut a vein and let it bleed;
nor the observing of peculiar light,
ringed round with what refractions peace can bring—
give it up, phrase-maker! your note is nothing:
the sum is everything.

Who walks attended by delight will feel it,
whom sudden sorrow hushes, he will know.
But you, who mark the drooping of an eyelid
or in a wrinkled cheek set out a reason—
sainted! But only if you see—

                              and only then—

why, that the sum of all your notes is nothing . . .
Make a rich note of this—and start again.

XLVIII

Surround the thing with phrases, and perceptions;
master it with all that muscle gives
of mastery to mind,—all strengths, all graces,
flexes and hardnesses; the hand, the foot;

quick touch of delight, recoil of disgust;
and the deep anguish too, the profound anguish,
which bursts its giddy phrase. Surround the thing
with the whole body's wisdom, the whole body's
cunning, all that the fingers have found out,
the palm touched of smoothness or roughness;
the face felt, of coolness or stillness;
the eye known, of mystery in darkness;
the ear found in silence.

Surround the thing with words, mark the thing out
passionately, with all your gestures become words,
patiently, with all your caution become words,
your body a single phrase—

                  And what do you say—?
O simple animal, twisted by simple light—!
do you tell space or time what the thing is?
Or do you tell the 'thing' that it is you!

L

And the child said to me in a dream—
habitual strength is no stronger than habitual weakness:
the habitual hero is no hero:
the habitual weakling has found his marvellous level:
who knows, for another, good from evil?
the only strong one is the angel who is half devil.

And then I stooped, and saw
under our footsteps the imponderable law,
the vast and shapeless and bloodbeating Thing—
inestimable ruin which conceived a wing.
unspeakable glory which conceived a claw—
and hung my head in shame
that I should blame
these indecipherable and unintelligible notes
scrawled on the nearest margin of the world—
these mites, these men, these motes.

LI

The miracle said 'I' and then was still,
lost in the wing-bright sphere of his own wonder:
as if the river paused to say a river,
or thunder to self said thunder.

As once the voice had spoken, now the mind
uttered itself, and gave itself a name;
and in the instant all was changed, the world
two separate worlds became—

The indivisible unalterably divided;
the rock forever sundered from the eye;
henceforth the lonely self, by self anointed,
hostile to earth and sky.

Alas, good angel, loneliest of heroes!
pity your coward children, who become
afraid of loneliness, and long for rock
as sick men long for home.

LVIII

Why should we care what this absurd child does,
follow him idly, watch the doll
laid in the grass and covered with dead leaves—
fingers tenderly lacing the dead leaves—
pathetic solicitude of the foolish for the unknowing?
why should we stand here, and watch this travesty,
we, the wise and old, the hardened, the disillusioned
from our window of bright despair looking downward
at the little contemptible street of human affairs—
and the child there, unconscious, tender, preoccupied,
bending in the dust above his beloved fragment?

Or the old men and women going up and down:
those with tired feet, or bent hands; those who see

dimly before them as indeed dimly behind them:
who greet one another stupidly and kindly:
is this not too to be dreadfully despised,
that thus we stand, secretly, behind curtains,
pitying the children, who were ourselves,
and the old, who will be ourselves—
pitying and despising, who will ourselves be pitied and despised:
but feeling, in memory and foresight, a kind of power?

But what else can we do, we who wait here between
one wall and another one clock and another
who can neither play happily in the dust, nor lie still?
too late for the one, too soon for the other,
what can we do but hide behind curtains, and spy?
Spying joyfully on the two blessings, beginning and end?

LX

The chairback will cast a shadow on the white wall,
you can observe its shape, the square of paper
will receive and record the impulse of the pencil
and keep it too till time rubs it out
the seed will arrange as suits it the shape of the earth
to right or left thrusting, and the old clock
goes fast or slow as it rusts or is oiled.
These things or others for your consideration
these changes or others, these records
or others less permanent. Come if you will
to the sea's edge, the beach of hard sand,
notice how the wave designs itself in quick bubbles
the wave's ghost etched in bubbles and then gone,
froth of a suggestion, and then gone.
Notice too the path of the wind in a field of wheat,
the motion indicated. Notice in a mirror
how the lips smile, so little, and for so little while.
Notice how little, and how seldom, you notice
the movement of the eyes in your own face, reflection
of a moment's reflection. What were you thinking
to deliver to the glass this instant of change, what margin

belonged only to the expectation of echo
and was calculated perhaps to that end, what was left
essential or immortal?

          Your hand too,
gloved perhaps, encased, but none the less
already bone, already a skeleton,
sharp as a fingerpost that points to time—
what record does it leave, and where, what paper
does it inscribe with an immortal message?
where, and with what permanence, does it say 'I'?
Perhaps giving itself to the lover's hand
or in a farewell, or in a blow,
or in a theft, which will pay interest.
Perhaps in your own pocket, jingling coins,
or against a woman's breast. Perhaps holding
the pencil dictated by another's thought.

These things do not perplex, these things are simple,—
but what of the heart that wishes to survive change
and cannot, its love lost in confusions and dismay—?
what of the thought dispersed in its own algebras,
hypothesis proved fallacy? what of the will
which finds its aim unworthy? Are these, too, simple?

LXII

The bird flying past my head said previous previous
the clock too said previous
I was warned, I was too soon, but I went on
taking with me a buzzing headful of omens
as this, and that, and the other, all to no good
turn back, go to the right, no no go forward,
under that tree, under that cliff, through that man's house
his wife will tell you, ask her the way

I went and asked, it was all as I had foreseen,
one thing and then another all as if planned
the bird saying previous previous and the clock croaking
the cliff and the tree and the house and the wife

the husband looking askance at me over his work
why it is all a dream I said and hurried
with leaden or golden steps in dream's bravado
past bird clock cliff tree wife and husband

into the beyond—but what was the beyond but nothing
nothing nothing—a shore a shape a silence
an edge a falling off—a loaf of fog
sliced by a knife. It was then that I turned back,
and found the past was changed and strange as future—
cliff tree wife and husband changed and strange;
and the same or a different bird flew past my head
saying previous previous, as if I were again too soon.

LXIV

Insist on formality if you will, let the skeleton
insist on formality if it will
allow it the hat the spats the gloves
and let it observe its exquisite decorum
at weddings or funerals, even at christenings

Let it say yes and no and hum and haw
give it an eyeglass and a programme of the music
something to do with hand and eye
it will embrace you pat you on the back
say it remembers you and knew your father

Let it observe its exquisite decorum
in the manipulation of decay—
and sing too—with hearty sepulchral voice—
in celebration of those rituals
which make a formal of the absolute

As if it were better, at the end of time,
when time runs faster, to mark the minutes out
with gold or diamonds, even with cannonshot—
the intervals more regular and precise
—and decorated too—to give them dignity!

Precisely what is this? that we should face
with such a putting on of airs and gloves
the bone, already formal in itself?
as if to minimize or decorate
the bone in bone, the order of skeleton!

For god's sake men, for god's sake women,
let the wild love too have its moment
let us forget the bone that flesh is heir to
and be informal—if never again—
at weddings and funerals, if not at birth.

LXVI

Brought them with him and put them down, as if
to come from nowhere with a random burden
of odd and ends, and quids and quods and surds,
whatnots and whiches—as if to put them down
were tantamount to saying he had thought them
and thought the bringing and thought the putting down
and thought himself who thought he brought them there

as if such randomness were part of nature
as if such casualness were part of nature
or the mad separateness of such an action
whether it served a purpose or served none
were the precise bright plume of God's own madness

but not that either, no, a different thing—
the always bringing, the always putting down
the odds and ends and quids and quods and surds
but never new, never the bright beginning,
as if the beginning were always at the middle
and never rememberable the sunrise words

who was it brought them with him and put them down
who was it came from nowhere and dropped his burden
the nondescript purveyor of nondescriptions
exhausted speaker of the exhausted word

wind outblown the word that died with speaking
the helplessness of helpless thought.

LXVII

Walk man on the stage of your own imagining
peel an orange or dust your shoe, take from your pocket
the soiled handkerchief and blow your nose
as if it were indeed necessary to be natural
and speak too if an idea should recommend itself
speak to the large bright imaginary audience
that flattering multiplication of yourself
so handsomely deployed and so expectant
tell them between flingings of orange peel
or such other necessary details of your rôle
precisely what they are, or what you are
since—lamentably—they are so much the same thing.
Decrepit inheritor of the initial star!
do you yourself sometimes imagine
or even perhaps say to that peculiar audience
something of this? as that yourself and they
comprise one statement? supercilious
the actor may be, often is, to those who hear him
but to be supercilious to one's self
even in one's dramatic moments!—marvellous
decay of what in God's first declaration
might have been good.

LXVIII

What you have said and cannot say again
prevented word that would have said your pain
idea prevented by the forbidden word
deliver us from this, bright alphabet

what you have thought and cannot think again
prevented thought that would have found its word—
word prevented by the forbidden thought—
deliver us from this, deep alphabet

the word walks with us, is a ghost of word—
the thought walks with us, is a ghost of thought
thus to the world's end in a silence brought
and to a babel our dark alphabet

come heart, invent a new word a new thought:
feel with new heat, new brightness, *a* and *b*
may thus become a glass through which we'll see
new worlds lost in the old world's alphabet

the sudden light, the sudden breaking, the sudden whirl—
come light, come light, let the heart be a bird
whose single being is a single word
brightness beyond soul or alphabet.

LXIX

I saw all these things and they meant nothing
I touched all these hands and they meant nothing
I saw all these faces Lord and they meant nothing
Lord Zero they meant nothing

accept my worship Zero for these devotions
for all these sins and for their absolutions
remit my guilt and wash my hands Lord Zero
for yours was the conception

and I will teach you in another world
out of my misery I will learn and teach you
I will teach you Lord in another world
I will give you my heart

the heart that the sailor gives to the broken ship
or the wheelwright to the turning wheel
the heart that the farmer gives to the frozen furrow
a stubborn heart like that

and I will also teach you by giving you my hands
look how they are injured Lord, see how hard they are

see how their beauty has been marred and scarred
I will teach you by giving you my hands

Christ had not hands like these, his hands were perfect
Christ's heart was great, not small like mine,
I do not believe in Christ, he is our dream,
and you too are our dream, Lord Zero

but we will defeat you, we will convert you,
we will teach you to laugh as the unhappy do
you will become human and broken like ourselves
you will become One with us, Lord Zero

(It is here that the little doubt comes in from the window
like a cold wind fluttering the leaves
and we ourselves go forth again on that wind
to become Lord Zero.)

LXXIV

This flower, she said to the child, you may have,
this with the little veins in the throat, and this
white one with the three purple spots, this too
take in your hand and watch it fade, forget
how it stood in the grass and cast a shadow
before it died. But this other flower
no, that is for later, that must be saved,
it must be left here, clinging to the side of the star
like a child at his mother's breast,
with the plantain leaves at the right and the grassblades
crisscrossed about the cool strong stem, and the green acorn
lying on the earth beside it at the left.
Of this you may keep only what you remember.
And it will live still, with an intense light,
when the others are dead.

                    The child walked westward
with the whole evening round him like a bell,
clear and deep and full of stars, the slow fading
of the green twilight like a fading flower, the stars

brightening in the huge arch. He counted them,
turned in a circle and counted others, and still others,
saw how the lower were the larger and brighter,
then stood at fault; walked back to ask again;
but she was gone. Now he would never know
which one, of all these stars, now he would never know
which star it was the flower had clung to—
flower and star and voice were gone—;
while the whole evening seemed to him like a hand
defending him,—forbidding, but defending.
Yet in the darkness was something new, something bright,
which was neither in the cold grass at his feet
nor in the sky: it was the simple image
of the star with the flower on its breast;
this he could have, this he could keep.

LXXV

And that grin, the grin of the unfaithful,
the secret grin of self-congratulation
facing the mirror at midnight, when all has gone well,
when the returning footstep has not been heard,
nor the errand guessed, nor the change of heart perceived,
nor the eye's secret discovered, nor the rank perfume
smelled on hand or mouth

                        that grin like a flower
which opens voluptuously amid poisons and darkness
at the mere sight of itself as if to say
courage you have done it let now bravado
match in its brazenness the mercurial deception
go forth and kiss the cheek of her you have deceived
you too have known this and failed to be ashamed
have brazened it out and grinned at your own grin
holding the candle nearer that you might see
the essential horror.

                   Yes, and you have noted
how then the chemistry of the soul at midnight
secretes peculiar virtue from such poisons:

you have been pleased: rubbed metaphoric hands:
saying to yourself that the suffering, the shame,
the pity, and the self-pity, and the horror,
that all these things refine love's angel,
filth in flame made perfect.

LXXVIII

But having seen the shape, having heard
the voice, do not relate the phantom image
too nearly to yourself, leave the bright margin
between the text and page, a little room
for the unimagined. What's here, beneath your hand,
is less and more than what you see or feel;
deeper than air or water; deeper than thought
can dive, whether between stars or between gods;
deeper than the sound of your heart. Walk right or left
it is no matter, whether in room or field,
under a tree, beside a road, the shape
will be deciphered only to elude you.
Is the fog only the shape of yourself, idiot?
and the fog an idiot too? is the god
your own vast fog of folly projected?
Think better of your love than this!

                                  She reads a book:
her hands are on the table: the bright light
falls on the opened pages, the two pages,
and on the ordered words. And while she breathes
the braids upon her bosom rise and fall
as slowly as her eyes recite the lines,—
from left to right, from right to left, softly
reshaping from that sight a world of sound.
There with her ears, but not with ears, she learns
how leaves can make an aureate grace of air
weaving a visual pattern, but in sound;
moved by the wind, heard by the poet's ear,
and now in visual sign transcribed again.
What miracle is this? that she who reads
here in a simple room of time and chairs,

can watch a bough dissect an arc of sky?
can feel the current of the wind that lifts it?
can hear, and see, and feel, that wound in air?
As the bough dips and flurries, she reads and breathes;
as move the leaves, her hands upon the page;
as lives the tree, or as the poet lives
in living with the tree, so lives her eye;
and as the poem lives, her woman's grace.
But which lives first? and who is living?

                                          God
is such a margin as thus lies between
the poem and the page's edge, a space
between the known and the imagined, between
the reported and the real. He is your fancy.
And you are his.

LXXXI

Assurance can come from nothing, or almost nothing;
the imperceptible accretion of trifles;
the mistaken speech, acknowledged, or unacknowledged,
the penetration of a deception; it can come
from observation of what has been unobserved:
new knowledge of an old history, new sight
of a known face, a known field; the path
familiar to the foot, but with surprises,
a raw pebble, dislodged by rain, a scarlet leaf
drowned in a puddle, a branch of maple to brush the sleeve,
or such other casuals. It can come
with a change of weather, the sundrawn mist
exaggerating softly the shape of a tree, snow
altering the face of a house, so that you guess
but do not know, yet triumph in knowing. Or can come,
and this is best, from the renewed inspection
of a known thing, and long loved; something small,
something tiny, but loved. The pimpernel,
hidden, with dusty petals, in deep grass,
obscure but always remembered, clear and

delicate, but with something obtuse as well,
obtuse and infinitesimal—this is the sort
of well-loving, and well-knowing, that changes
Tuesday to Wednesday.

Why not, or why,
have Wednesday for Tuesday? This is a question
which neither the heart nor calendar can answer.
But if assurance can feed itself on change,
change, then, and be assured.

LXXXIII

Music will more nimbly move
than quick wit can order word
words can point or speaking prove
but music heard

How with successions it can take
time in change and change in time
and all reorder, all remake
with no recourse to rhyme!

Let us in joy, let us in love,
surrender speech to music, tell
what music so much more can prove
nor talking say so well:

Love with delight may move away
love with delight may forward come
or else will hesitate and stay
finger at lip, at home,

But verse can never say these things;
only in music may be heard
the subtle touching of such strings.
never in word.

LXXXIV

What face she put on it, we will not discuss:
she went hence an hour since. Where she went,
is another matter. To the north, to the south,
as the man whistled, or the whim bade, she went,
or even—who can say—following a star.
Her heart is like an hourglass, from which the sand runs—
no sooner run than tilted to run again;
her mind, a mirror, which reflects the last moment;
her face, you would know it anywhere, it gives you back
your own light, like the moon. Tell her a lie,
threefold she reflects it; tell her the truth,
and its returned brilliance will strike you dead.
She is of quicksilver. You might as well
pillow your head on a cloud, as on that breast,
or strive to sleep with a meteor: when you wake,
she is gone, your own hand is under your cheek.

Yet she is of the material that earth is made of:
will breed as quick as a fly; bloom like the cherry,
fearless of frost: and has a nimble fancy
as tropic in pattern as a fernleaf. She walks
as naturally as a young tree might walk:
with no pretence: picks up her roots and goes
out of your world, and into the secret darkness,
as a lady with lifted train will leave a ballroom,
and who knows why.

                    Wherefor do you love her, gentlemen?
Because, like the spring earth, she is fruitfulness?
and you are seed? you need no other reason?
and she no other than her perpetual season.

LXXXV

Observe yourself, but placidly: the mirror
is well placed, with the light behind you: Narcissus

could ask no more. This is the face you shave,
at morning, tenderly, with care for moles
or small excrescences more temporal:
you know, have felt, time and again, its cheeks,
their roughnesses and hollows; the fat chin;
the corners of the mouth, each different;
one melancholy, one weak. You know the eyes,
the faded blue, which cannot meet your gaze,
and the drooped eyelid, after dissipation,
hung low upon a large unseeing pupil.
The earlobes too you love, your fingers love—
scooped, like the nostrils, for crisp lather; the nose,
you disregard, provided it can breathe.
The brow—what of the brow? You press your hand
against that span of bone and flesh, to feel
its ache grow deeper, if it aches; the bone
resists the hand, with deep surprise to both,
that its own hand should rise against the brain.
And the hand wonders what the sore brain thinks.

The hand wonders, but the dull eye also:
questions the mirrored eye and eyelid: stares
more painfully, in that glazed and lidded pupil,
than ever proud Narcissus in his pool.
What's there? what virtue, or what truth? Hatred
glares back at you; the dulled eye is stupid;
but not too stupid, or too dull, for hate.
You hate each other; you lean and hate; the light
shows deeply into hate. Who is that man?
His face is meanness, and should be destroyed!
But then the mouth—

     For suddenly the mouth
begins to smile; and smiles and smiles; and grins
maudlin affection; unless it be divine.
Is it divine? or maudlin? The two faces
glare at each other; sober; become still.
There is a truce, there is a silence: you lean
toward each other, into mystery.

Who is that man? His face is strange, and good!
unknown, and therefor god . . .

                    And so, once more,
eternity makes heartbreak peace with time.

LXXXVIII

And look and remember well, as with an actor,
how each moment is that brilliant and particular
stepping forward from shadow to the stage
where all will be seen; the lights are beneath you
and beyond the lights the crowd, a silence;
so that the flexing of your knee is noted;
the arch of your hand, or the turn of your cheek
burned away from you as soon as seen.
The eyelid droops only to be torn from you;
your smile, your tears, our heart,
exist only to be devoured. Courage
must bear you swiftly, each moment must carry you
to the next safe gesture: each expression
must take you quickly from the last, it is a race
with anonymous hatred and innumerable eyes.
What you were, they have eaten, and already
they eat what you are. You must hurry
like a magician from trick to trick; the smile
is flung like a handkerchief, the frown is dropped
rapidly to take its place, next you must turn
with a dancer's grace, angrily
stoop to tie a shoelace, or else again
stand with your finger to chin as in thought.
It is all seen, it is all eaten, nothing
escapes that mouth of hungry light, only
the extreme of agility and practice will find you
a safe exit into the wings.
If applauded, perhaps you have been a practiced actor;
swift in mimicry, an adjustable ape,
quick as a typewriter or a telegraph,
and perhaps no better. If received in silence,
it may be that you were an honest man.

XCII

But no, the familiar symbol, as that the
curtain lifts on a current of air, the rain
drips at the window, the green leaves seen in the
lamplight are bright against the darkness, these
will no longer serve your appetite, you must have
something fresh, something sharp—

The coarse grassblade, such as will cut
a careless finger, the silver pencil
lying straight along the crack in the table
in its pure rondure a multitude of reflections
or else your own thumbnail suddenly seen
and as if for the first time

Strongly ridged, warm-coloured as flesh but cool,
the pale moon at the base, and the fleck of scar
which grows slowly towards the tip—you think of a river
down which a single dead leaf perhaps is carried
or you think of a glacier in which
an acorn has been frozen—

But these too are familiar, it is not these
which will say your thought, you lift desperately
your eyes to the wall—the smooth surface
awaits them as precisely and coldly
as the paper awaits the gleaming pencil, giving
nothing, not even a resistance—

Where will you turn now if not to the rain,
to the curtain in the wind, the leaf tapping the window,
these are the wilderness, these are beyond
your pencil with its reflections
your thumbnail with its suggestion of rivers and glaciers
now you must go abroad

To the wild night which everywhere awaits you
and the deep darkness full of sounds

to the deep terror in which shines for a moment
a single light, far-off, which is suddenly quenched
this is the meaning for which you seek a phrase
this is your phrase.

XCVI

It is the other, it is the separate, it is the one
whose touch was strange, who with an eyeglance
sounded and wounded you, who went then
quickly to another world, who was gone
before you had guessed, before you had known,
quick as the shadow of a whip over grass
or the shadow of falling water on a rock—
he who said yes, but with a separate meaning,
who said no with an air of profound acceptance,
he who was other, he who was separate—

That precious thing is gone, that bright grassblade
suddenly by the frost's fierce tongue
was silvered and melted, how will you have it back—
there is no having it unless you had it,
lament your selfishness in vain, be sentimental
and hug the lost image, it is in vain,
he remains in another world—

                    Simple one, simpleton,
when will you learn the flower's simplicity—
lie open to all comers, permit yourself
to be rifled—fruitfully too—by other selves?
Self, and other self—permit them, permit them—
it is summer still, winter can do no more
who brings them together in death, let them come
murderously now together, it is the lifelong
season of meeting, speak your secret.

Landscape West of Eden

It was of a deck, the prow of a ship, uplifted
by the wide wave of blue and whiteness, swung
towards the star-side by a long wave from the west,
then earthward dropped. And there I, not alone,
westward facing,

          and with me the two children,
Eve and Adam, from Eden come with flowerbuds,
and roots of flowers, and acorns in their hands,
and words for worms and flies; and the long slow sunset
bridled the redfoamed sea, from north across to south,
touching each wavetop with a crimson feather,
and the seabirds too were red;

            and as I lay, rising and falling
as rose the crimsoned waterwaves, remembering
seas, seas, and other seas, and seas before them,
above earth, under, and in this kind of dream,—
and those too fainter that with waves of less than nothing
chill the faint cheeks of stars,—so I watched
how, in a later age, the long clouds of brilliant scarlet
with openings of light from the last lost sun
were but as trains of human purpose, that weakly cross
from one frail island to another island, farther.
And so I said (but Eve and Adam were silent):
'It is the death and daybreak, all in one;
sow your seeds in the dark, and they will prosper.'

I smiled at them, but they smiled not at me.
They held with small hard hands their buds and flowers
and precious seeds from Eden,—but how could they believe
—poor darlings, angels of the daybreak! how could they think

to plant the bright gold solid seeds of Eden, and the bright shoots,
in something less than Eden or more than earth?

Nor could I persuade them; nor, not being God, would wish
to alter the inalterable, save for my own poor pleasure,
—and that perhaps were pleasure enough? to see the change
alter historic eyes, with all the fallen stars removed?
the constellations clearer, those I know?
But ah, poor children, to make them the victims
of such ideal delight! that they should see their flowers
wither, or worse, worse still, grow to strange shapes!
And am I a father, that I should beat my children for this?
No, no, my darlings, do your murder in your own way,
as I in mine; and at the end of the world's evening,
when the harvest of stars has been gathered and stored for nothing
then we will sit together, and understand, and exchange
the husks of seeds which we vainly planted under the rainbow;
and you will say, 'You went farther,' and I will say,
'But to no purpose' . . .

                    But now we sail
westward together, and say nothing, hostile to each other,
and the world is good, and old, and deep.

                    II

And then the minstrel fellow, whom I hated,
came softly stepping, harp in hand, from wave to wave,
with such a brightness, such a lightness, such delight
in his own wave-flight across seas of chaos,
and such assurance, and such eyes of wisdom's colour,
and wings of the sea-eagle or the angel,
touching his heart to such deep chords of heaven-praise,
that I was ashamed, but also jealous. And I saw
how well and swiftly from wave to wave he came,
making such sport of it as swallow makes of summer-flight
for his own joy in motion. And 'O curst man,' he sang,
'you will know nothing, you will waste your life
in desperate voyages to the unknown coasts,—
turn back and listen; but you cannot, cannot listen;
nor, if you listened, could I sing to you with such power.'

Poised then upon the prow a moment, westward pointing,
his eyes contemptuous of the west as of the east,
he struck his heart and sang a southward song.
What comfort there? And Eve and Adam heard him, smiling,—
dear children, how they loved that sweetest heaven-praise!
And I too loved it, and I wept, but still I looked
beyond his heart and harp and wings to westward;
but for no reason, save my purpose there.

And southward then he flew, from crimson wave to wave,
with such a lightness, such delight, such heavenly brightness,
his eagle wings spread out in fiery light,
and in the winds of heaven his heart-harp making songs
of such divine and sorrowful home-going
as might have turned the ship's prow southward too.
But I too, like the children, Adam and Eve,
held in hard hands my stubborn seeds and shoots;
and closed my ears and eyes; and sailed to the shoreless
sunset land whose cliffs were only clouds.

III

And this dream-ship dissolved into evening light,
galleys of gold and crimson galleons and fiery caravels
sunk and consumed in fire with wrack of red clouds,
and the one island left that was myself—
this sunset-thought, here at the western window, looking
across the red marsh, where the dark birds fly homeward
athwart the day-end light,—as now my thoughts
bring back those images of Eve and Adam
to me once more, who sent them forth; and the angel too
who was myself come home.

                    The little road, far off,
turns up the hill, winding among tall trees,
loses itself among black shadowed houses
and there, forthgoing from the window in my thought's power,
I climb the hill in sunset light, going westward;
but soon my purpose flags, or I forget it;
and here again am standing before the open window,
remembering.

Remembering the 'out there' and the 'here within,'
this little coral island of the mind,
broken upon with all the foams of nescience;
now bared and glittering, now almost overwhelmed and drowned;
with its little memories of weeds, mosses, shells and sands,
left for a moment between one wave and other,
felt, noticed, hardly known through the hardness,
and swept away again.

Remembering also
the memories of these things, and the deep magic
wrought upon them by the falsenesses of memory:
the shell become a jewel, the sand become a desert,
the waves become the ineluctable hatred of chaos,
the weeds and mosses become as bridges of delight
wonderfully windswept, archangelically designed,
fairylifted and void-defying, between
one fever of darkness and the next; whereover
nimbly I send my messengers, and they return, swiftly,
with that fantastic nonsense which feeds the soul.

Thou art, thou art, thou hast, thou hast—
miraculously nothing, that miracle
which breathes out life and breathes in death;
say no more of it then than this, lost island soul,
no more than this; thou art and hast.

IV

But in the friendly night, walking in night's womb,
to first warm darkness again born back, and gladly
comforted by the mother-dark, feeling
the thick pulse, the cord of stars, and the far heart
beating its slow and heavy disatole
so that my being trembled, well knowing itself
to be where it was, and nowhere else, to be
the dull half-anguished resistance-joy of being:
and on the soft path walking toward a faint light
heartless myself but needing no heart, and following
the quick lights of firefly memories, gone and come,
so close that they touched me as I moved—

what need 1 more than this,
what need I, laughter, more than this,—you, voice of weeping,
what need I more than this? Then the angel with the lantern
held his light against my eyes so that I shrank back,
my eyes hurt by the cold full horror of light,
but too late turning back, for the light held me.
And he with hard strong hands grasped me and drew me forth
under the question of his lantern, marking
with shrewd eyes, my eyes, what my answers were.
'And come, coward,' he said, 'learn to give another answer
than pain! Learn how to dishevel the simplicities,
and to rejoice in the bitter dishevelment!'
And so I went with him, bewildered, to a mean room
squared out of time and space, and with their coldness,
and saw, for the first time, the almighty clock.

            V

The morning oak I praised, whose wide grey branches spread
hardily against a sky of blue and white
dipping his leaves to the wind and a frolic of rain
and in this summer-season as tolerant of jackdaws
as in the winter of snow. In the deep grass I stood,
under the singing circle of leaves and lichens,
watching the alternate colours of sky go over,
and hearing and feeling the wind among my flashing leaves:
raising the eastern boughs, and solemnly dipping the western;
whirling concentric a moment, and then still.
O mindless delight! the words had half escaped me,
as the oak too half escaped me: but the shadow
shifted and caught me, and I stood in shade to my knees,
remembering the foursquare room, and all my roots.

Then, when the wind pulled, I pulled a rock,
then gave a handful of leaves, a patter of acorns,
wasted on rock, or doomed to be stifled in grass;
and, the wind shifting, pulled at another rock,
gave him a branch of fresh-torn leaves and mast,
felt the birds gone. Is this the dishevelment
foreseen?

But I am walking again
naked of thought as an angel without wings, rejoicing
at nothing, or rejoicing that one can so rejoice
at nothing, and I am already again in my cold room
where now the oak-tree bursts the walls and ceiling.
Clock, here's an acorn for you! Here will be oaks.
Adam and Eve, dear children, will sit beneath you gladly
and tell each other the lovely lies of Eden;
while I, their humble father, ignored, will lean from the window,
and send to the sunset a powerful thought of death.

VI

Nevertheless, my dilapidated angel-self, with ragged wings,
pursued my flight into the far too purple west
and brought me back laughing from the sentimental sunset,
and slapped my hands to make them let go of the dirt of death,
and stood me in a corner, still laughing, and walked to and fro
half beating his wings, so that the room was windy;
and I, the oak-tree, whispered, and gave him two leaves.
'You, with your powerful sunset thought of death!' he said,
'You always westward going, as if in the west alone
the rainbow buried its golden claws! you with this longing
for many-coloured annihilation, sacrifice
for something, everything, or even nothing, if only
you go there with wings and come back with a halo!
why, are we so desperate yet? Must we die suddenly?
or is the North Star hero of a melodrama?
Is paper snow falling from the empyrean
on your poor soul, cast as the abandoned heroine?
Must we have bells and cannons and trumpets
and flowers flung for bones, garlands for skeletons,
harp-songs for *rigor mortis*? This were an insult to us.
Let us be quiet, and examine the causes as we may;
the rainbow's foot is in dishevelment;
the veriest fools and idiots can recognize the novel;
only the gods can know and praise the good.
And we are gods.'

Whereat I dissembled chagrin,
from this, my angel self, I concealed my sorest shame,
and for a while pretended to be a mindless tree.
Beneath me the two children exchanged trinkets of trove,
and kissed many times with increasing boldness,
and began, without knowing it, to plan a world.
I too was as simple as that: I could have moved
at one step into the fruitful south of worldmake
and spawned a rainbowed world like any fish.
Nor was the impulse lacking. I looked forth greedily
and saw where best this new magnificence might be:
there, there, it was; not shaped like any other world;
never before conceived as now my blood conceived it;
but now checked, with hatred, contempt, affection and laughter.
'Look!' I said to Eve and Adam, 'there is a world lost!'

And the satirical angel, with brightened wings, glowing,
with wisdom-coloured eyes, and a delightful stillness, said:
'We are still far from wisdom, still with pain and joy
accept the pure simplicities of the soul.'

VII

Sleepless lying many nights I thought of these things,
humble, hopeless yet, but with the mind's godlike eye
seeing always farther and deeper into the night-world,
myself seen also in a little hammock, swung
darkly parallel with the earth's dark surface,
absurd cocoon of consciousness, hung in the void,
ridiculous little worm-prism of the darkly known.
With my hand I reached then upward and took Polaris
and flung him southward into the night, there to start
a new world, and to leave the old world new;
now should be no more north for prophets and mariners.
And I scattered the Seven Sisters, so that I might laugh
watching them run like lost ants hither and thither
—but all this in a dream.

                    It was myself I thus dispersed,
thus with a thought altered to new pattern

for the delight in change, and the delight in knowing
the old order now forever fixed and inalterable;
fixed in the memory, but changed by thought of change;
for nothing changes but thinking makes it change.
As one would move the vases on the mantelpiece,
the right to left, the left to right; and shift the clock,
and perhaps also shift its meaningless measure of time,
so that this profound void interval we call a second
has become instead a long and transverse wind,
a tide of space; down which we altered plunge
to a new knowledge of sublime forgetfulness.
Then, like angelic salmon, to reascend
up the long cataract of strange re-ordered order,
to a new shape of dream, a new design of God.
So, having moved the vases (only with a thought of moving)
and made the clock (which was an ear) an eye,
the room grown shapeless, and myself shapeless, then
delighted came I back to the world of memory;
as a swimmer, long submerged, beaten by waves,
comes up at last triumphant from long darkness,
and sees the cliffs above him, and his own tree,
birds with white bright feathers, the shore of warm pebbles,
an oak leaf, close to his cheek, in sea-froth, whirling,
the seal shining on the wet rock, and all these things
vivid and hard as metal in the bright sunlight;
and himself too as hard and clear as they.

Thus I renewed
the world within, the world without, world without end.

VIII

Not for long will man walk in this world
before death speaks to him and dread deflects him
from child's delight in flowers; and time is doom,
and sounds and sights of dolour, come with the clucking clock,
strike the heart's midnight. Nor is it far,
as ravens and buzzards fly, from the cradle to the grave.
Thou hast, thou art, and then thou hast not, art not.
Look how the sunlight blazes on red blooms

whether they be in garden, or in field, or in the mind,
or on the undiscoverable and unremembered grave.
And thus I saw (walking forth) the crumbling stones
heavy with honeysuckle; and forthwith I remembered,
though still a child, the bones that gave me birth.

This was the west wind, over flowers, that softly came
whispering whys and whithers, wherefrom I went
kneedeep in goldenrod and became drunk with sun.
There the first angel came, flying from tomb to tomb,
winnowing grass and flowers, slowly, with indifferent wings,
and followed, smiling, as I went in doubt from stone to stone,
perching on each in turn, and holding in his hand
a withered flower. And at first I avoided him
and moved away, ashamed, and with sly pretence of leisure
went to another grave, another tomb, another vault,
and saw the bones.

          And then he gave me
the withered flower, and this I held in my hand,
stared at, and thought long, and it was he
who spoke. 'This is your father,' he said, 'this is your mother,
and here are east and west, and downward-flowing water,
and the upward-going thought!'

              And thereupon I pondered
of upward-going thought; and cast away the flower;
and deep in hot goldenrod buried my face and wept;
and thrust my hands amid the stalks and earth.

IX

Spreading my boughs above the children, Eve and Adam,
the daylight warm and windless, and wisdom yet
not come to find the peril in wisdom's source,
they sleeping, he with pebbles in his hands, and she
with daisies in her hands, and in her hair—
so, with deliberate dream, I foresaw god.
It was as clear a feeling, and as cool,
as east wind brings to underside of oak-leaf,

precise and precious, dislodging raindrops,
and making ants to stumble . . . Dreaming thus I saw
the god of wrong, the downward-going god, which Eve and Adam
were doomed to be; and for myself alas I saw
the upward-going thought, but powerless to change these guilty
    lives.

    But from this vision waking
I spoke to them, walking angrily before them,
and asked them (who were ashamed and frightened)
whether they were awake, and what they knew of god,
and which of us was god, and which of us least godlike,
and whether indeed (considering all things)
we needed gods at all.

    Far off I saw the angel,
no larger than a mosquito above the trees;
and with discomfort I knew (but concealed it from the children)
the satiric laughter in his wisdom-coloured eyes.
And so I walked apart, my questions unanswered,
and left them puzzled, with the flowers and the pebbles,
and waited, in the little darkness of my own chagrin,
to see if he would come. And he came lightly,
but not derisively, nor with satire, rather with pity,
and this I suffered more; and before me, gravely,
stood for a moment silent, and then softly asked
which of us was god and which of us least godlike
and (if we needed gods) where we might find them?
Nor did he smile then; nor did I answer; and we stood
face to face for a long time, my eyes downcast
and his unwavering; until at last
I looked at him; and then he smiled, and as he smiled
I knew myself forgiven and foreseen, and my foreknowing
foreknown, and all the world I knew foredoomed.

    x

Ignorant I pitied myself, I went humbly
among stupendous fanfares and hornblasts of wisdom,
and none there were who knew less than I, and many

who sent their words with flags to the very ramparts of time.
Only the questioner I loved, the hemlock-lover,
him whom bitterness made sweet and humbleness made wise;
and not that poet who thought himself (alas) a god.
This much I learned from the tomb-seeing angel.
And this too I concealed from the children.

                                       And as I sat
there with the publican drinking bitter beer,
while the coarse clock ticked centuries for stupid stars,
calendars coming and going from dying printers of words,
planets cooling and changing as men change minds,
it was there the two men came from east and west,
wise men from west and east, and spoke their wisdom;
while the publican with wings laughed in the corner.

And first the first one said, his face like sea-moss,
his hands the claws of gulls: 'Good fellow, I have been,
from here to there, from dust to water, and have known
all languages, and spoken them, and known also
the god withheld in each, the wisdom lost; but lastly
found, at the end of life—as now I am—this wonder:
this tongue, in which the meaning is so dispersed,
into such tiny particles, such fragments
of meaningless glitter, such infinitesimal surds,
that (on a careful estimate) it will take
a thousand years to assemble (of such sounds)
enough to make one meaning . . .'

                        Hearing this, I went forth and laboured
a thousand years; and slowly gathered, in my carts and barrows,
at last enough of sounds to make a meaning.
Proudly I brought them back, before the publican, and drank
his bitter beer again; and now the second sage
had just begun to speak. He pulled his beard, and said
(gently scorning the other sage, and also scorning
the carts and barrows which had brought my meaning):
'So say you? . . . Why, this is nothing. I have been
from there to here, and here to there, and found
at last the tongue of tongues; now, at the end of life, I know
what no philogist has known before me.'

At this the publican laughed, beating his wings,
'And what is this?' he said, 'another wonder?
One more of these, by God, and we shall have no sense, no sense
    at all!'
But the sage answered:

                        'It is a language
in which the meaning is so concentrated, so terrible, so godlike!—
that one quick syllable is a thousand years.'

And with that clap of thunder we were changed.

                XI

Nevertheless many times temptation of wisdom-pride
came to me, nor perhaps will I ever escape
that shameful fault, which is the folly of all fools;
as one day in the garden, under a tree, sleeping,
I woke and heard the voices of Eve and Adam beneath me.
They lay in languor, by love exhausted, laughing,
and idly (thinking me asleep) began to talk.
And Adam said: 'But if there are these things, Eve,—
the things we know, and know delightful,—may there not be
outside us, and beyond, in another world,
things more delightful still?'

                    I partly opened my eyes,
and watched how Eve, sitting in grass with idle hands,
touched in her thought, with those small hands relaxed,
unimagined wonders, in a world as yet unknown.
Sombre, with downcast eyes, she thought of these;
effortful; and with deliberate puzzlement;
and said: 'But Adam; who knows; may it not be
the new things might be dreadful?'

                        'Foolish woman!' he said,
'perhaps they are. Perhaps they are! But even so
(not that I think it likely) we could come
homeward again; if there are terrors in that world,—

devils, goblins, ghosts, the seven-sworded rainbow,
or ice that kills the heart,—think, think, how escaping these,
this garden would rejoice us!'

                    Thereupon I awoke,
and walked before them with my accustomed anger,
turning my back for a moment, only to glare at them between the
        leaves,
contemptuous as much of Adam's childish boldness
as of Eve's timidity and tenderness. Will I never learn
the wisdom that is aware, and watches, and gladly waits?
But I was impatient, and chided their impertinence,
and their small foolish foresight. 'Why!' I said,—
'What can you know of life, who are not yet dead?'
And then I boasted of all my bales and blessings,
my many times repeated death, wisdom of tombs,
horrors of chaos from which, again and again,
emerging godlike I made a man-shape of my misery.
'What can you know, who are young as the yellow primrose?
Will you cast horoscopes at the age of pollen?
Learn first to wither!'

                As I walked, I watched warily,
for fear my sceptic angel might in secret slyness
be hiding near. It was not he, but Adam,
who chastened me. For Adam said:

                            'Forgive my foolishness,—
but is not pollen the seed of dead plants, and of death?'

Then suddenly, before him, I was ashamed.
For in his eyes, lowered, abashed, I clearly saw
wisdom and innocence, and innocence in wisdom,
the death of shame; and knew him destined, in his time,
to be my angel . . .

But I was proud, and turned my back, and said no word.

XII

Were one to know the world as a wide wanhope of web
such as with shrouded eye the hornet sees, when death-caught,
then, when he hears only the humming of his own wingbeat,
naught answering, naught pitying, no reply
from hornet-gods,—only the dreadful silent shape
approaching abruptly, he, the enemy, the unknown—
why this were something, too, to know, this plane of silken
treachery, in which the wing is worse than worthless!
Are gods exempt? is the cold cloud exempt? the wind,
is he exempt? At sunset the wind dies, slowly,
the cold cloud dies of snow, the world is a tomb
of dead gods. But this is simple, this simplicity
of cruelty, intelligible and terrible,
godlike and therefor good!

                    Thus, as I watched the water
on a black night of bitter star and frost,
first freezing in small fans and ferns of glass,
clicking and tinkling, then with sullen creakings closing,—
the leaf encased, the floating twig, the stick, the straw,
at the white edge the pebbles too embraced in claws of ice—
and, at last, groaning, the whole pond imprisoned—
thus, I thought of the many deaths and murders by which we
    live—
how one thought slays another, itself then slain;
and frost creeps over feelings, and time destroys
what frost has spared.

                    Above the hill I saw
the moon's dead beauty come; trees snapped in the cold,
wounded forever; and in my heart I knew
the children's quarrel, in which hard words are flung
and murder done in play, which will at last be earnest . . .
And so I clenched my murderous hands and laughed.

XIII

The peach-tree being in bloom, beneath it I waited,
centuries, between the falling of light pink petals;

one fell upon my hand, another in my hair;
one was dislodged by a sparrow, another by a bee;
a third the wind flung down; the fourth and fifth fell of their
own weight; and I awoke from sleep
to find the sixth beside me in warm grass.
Far off below me, on a long slope of hill, I saw various
new furrows in a field, sleeked by the ploughshare,
so that they glistened in the May sunlight,—
new waves of earth, and bright as waves of sea.
There the birds foraged, cried as they settled,
alarmed went chattering westward, where they waited;
till quiet came again, and they returned to earth.

But what I waited for, unless it were earth-wisdom,
or warm persuasion of the slow spring-season-sunlight;
or what the peach-tree blossoms (leisurely falling) had to say—
who will interpret this, in words of quartz and crystal?
laziness was my light, delight was less in laughter;
slow was the pulse, and penitent, for past foolishness;
pollen blood went frothily in my veins, and sluggishly;
and I lay still as tree-root . . .

                  I watched the cloud
(carved by the peach-tree into shapes no cloud should know),
pass slowly over, blossoms dark against its white,
westward; until it cleared the tree, and sank gravely
into the sunset and a red resurrection.
And I thought of Eve and Adam, changed by morning and
    evening;
myself, by the blossoms changed; blossom, by birdsong;
shadow, by time; and the heart happy with nonsense . . .
And so lay smiling until the seventh blossom fell.

    XIV

'Strange, strange it is,' I said to the dark angel—
he, darkened by his thought, as I by mine,
and as the field we sat in was darkened by a cloud—
'strange that the body should be unfaithful to the mind,
the mind unfaithful to the body! will the soul wander

witless among the waters and hills which are her own?
This peach-blossom is visited by innumerable
bees and flies and butterflies (faithless wantons);
it is their faithlessness that makes them welcome.
Thus, she is fertile; thus, the mind is fertile; why then
must love be sterile, in pure faithfulness?'

'Why indeed?' the angel said.

'Let Eve love Satan, and Adam adore Lilith then,' I answered:
'Eve will learn much from Satan, and Adam from Lilith,—
and how delicious, how new, this wisdom will be!
Satan disguising himself—needlessly—quite needlessly!—
as the insinuating, the insidious, the all-knowing serpent!
and Lilith—what will Lilith be? what will Lilith be?'

'Là, là!' the angel said.

'But then'—I pondered aloud—'will Eve love Adam? or Adam
love Eve? will they bring back their wisdoms?
will each receive from the other the new wisdoms?
will they be angry?'

'They will be angry,' the angel said.

'Ah! Just as I thought! . . . Rain is unfaithful to field,
ocean to air, lover to lover,
mind to body and body to mind. The thought
runs westward, while the body leches eastward!
Thought will want fractions, body will want flesh!
Here are no conclusions?'

'Thou sayest it? Thou knowest? Then thou growest!
And soon, thou wilt learn to laugh.'

Whereat he rose, and spread angelic wings,
and eastward went to Eden; while in the grass I wondered
at the disparateness—or so it seemed—of thought and flesh;
and held the blossom in my hand, and in a vision
saw the world ending in a laughter of pure delight.

XV

The tired hand, the tired eye,—these too will have place
in thought's constellation, which sags slowly
earthward and sleepward, and as it sinks grows brighter,
brighter and larger; so grow the setting stars,
magnified to magnificence in earth's miasma.
Thus fever inflames the infinitesimal;
the seed becomes a world, terrors become gods;
and thus fatigue makes prophecies and portents
of its own weariness.

        Or so I thought, while evening
brightened above the marsh-mist the first planet-light;
and, tired, I felt my tiredness turn to tired thought;
tired thought to sadness; sadness to bitter despair,
despair to wisdom, backward-looking, but such wisdom
as lives on nightshade, and the moonlight in waste places.
Ruin of thought? ruin of gods and worlds? ruin
of man's brief empire?

        I saw Adam sleeping, Eve
sleeping beside him; her hand was on his shoulder,
the buttercups half-fallen from it, some of them fallen,
behind him fallen, her hand relaxed and sleeping too—
and Adam's hand, asleep also, was on her hip;
the caress arrested, poised, postponed. And so they waited
(not knowing that they waited) for the renewal
of loves exhausted, and beliefs destroyed.
But in the morning—how new their love would be!
the world, how young! the buttercups, how many!
and Eve so strange to Adam, and Adam so strange to Eve!

Where then,—I said to the moon,—is honesty?
can thought be trusted, if it change its tune
as weariness, or weather, time or space or mood,
dictate the theme? If so, here's chaos come.
If thought must change, as changing seasons change,
change to the dictates of the blood and moon, the mind
moving to measures of the mere unmeaning—

is honesty the best policy, or policy
the only honesty? Surely the latter, like a bright fixed star,
will guide us firmly, ineluctably,
variants overruled, safely to nowhere?
Choosing a thought, we'll sail to it, and die,—
somewhere between the thought and nought . . . But if
we choose for honesty itself, why then, we'll change
minute by minute the bewildered compass;
we'll change our minds, as change our moods; and die still
    changing.
And wisdom will be change, and faith in change . . .

Thus in the evening, as I watched the moon enlarge,
westward sinking, with a rim of golden cloud,
myself went westward too, in enlarged thought;
and sank in somnolent magnificence, slowly,
in grandiose gradualness, to divinest sleep.

      XVI

'Daybreak?' the angel said. 'But what is daybreak, god?
do you mean night-break? do you mean dark-break?
or else, poor dreamer, do you mean that sullen waking
from sleep's omniscient nescience to sad thought?
Why, would you have, flung from the eastern mountain-top,
three stars, an arrow of light, and a rose-petal?
Is this so precious? is this a harbinger of joy?
O come and climb with me; eastward we fare from Eden;
thus we will speed the dawn; and thus—ah, think of this—
will speed the sunset too.'

                  He spread angelic wings,
wide as the valley seemed they in the darkness, beating,
and whirled the air and rose; and with him, I, unwilling,
beat my new wings, which ill sustained me eastward,
already burdened with foredoom and feel of night.
Eastward we went, and Eden fell behind us;
until our eastward thought so far outran us
that we were there, before our wings were there.
Hung on our wings, then, in the empyrean,

we waited, for such dawn as never comes.
And as we hung there, in the foreday whisper,
the first warm currents of air intermingling with the cold,
the birds beneath us singing in still-dark trees,
he said, and smiled:

              'Mortal god, it is given to no mortal
to see his birth. Go further eastward yet;
your birth is still before you. Seek it, yes!
ah, my friend, though there is warmth in sunrise; it is not such
as warms the hand; and if it warms the heart,
or gives the mind's eye vision, or brings comfort
to those weak gods who long to know their birth,
it gives no joy to you.'

              Thereat he turned,
and westward went; easily; with slow wingbeat, floating
on westward flowing light. For now the sun
had thrust a golden limb above the mountain-top;
and all the eastern trees were edged with brightness,
and my own wings were bright before my eyes;
so bright that all the east was dim with light;
and that dark world, from which I came, obscured.
Marvellous was it, warm in colour, rose-bright, and deep;
wonders came up from it, whirling, and went westward;
the sun rose, the earth and stars all changed,
my wings I stilled, eastward eagerly staring.
But though I saw the gashes of bright light,
the depths of terror, the void, the vividness, the wonder,
horror of trees outlined against the brightness,
I saw no more.

          And so at last, wiser only
in facing the unknown, I flew past Eden.

XVII

And then the minstrel fellow, whom I hated,
him of the harp, the Hermes-heeled, the southward
sybarite, wide-winged, and with such case of flight
as made my new wings heavy, came from the south,

touching angelic laughter from his heart-strings,
so sweet a song that all the birds were still.
Then, beneath the shadow of his wider wings,
shadowed by them, and sheltered, and also shamed,
and in the stillness hung beneath him, hearing
his heavenly voice, I held my speech, and speechless
waited until he spoke.

              'O infant god,' he said,
'empty-handed you come from east and west,
took not my warning, followed me not,
saw not, or heeded not, the wisdom-colour of my eyes,
nor heard my song; heed now, and bend your flight
southward with me, and sleep in heart-warmth there.'

Softly the song fell, his shadow against the sun
was cool and great, nor would it have been hard
to follow in his wake, when, with slow measure,
he separated light from dark, and flew
southward once more; and from him, as he went,
came the soft harp-strings of his southern heart.
With even flight he flew, and left the sky
as cold and bright above me as before;
no shadow sheltered me; so that I longed
to go with him, as longed my wings to follow
the current of his wings; which still, in the cold air,
fanned at my feathers.

             But I hung still, above
the oak-tree; and beneath the oak-tree saw
Adam and Eve, whose eyes were eastward turned.

XVIII

Thus from the window eastward faring in thought I went,
no longer now by footpaths humbly content to go
but spreading imagination's widening wings;
and saw the origin, the east-light, the red daybreak,
the void of the unknowable, whence we come.
And must we know—I thought sadly—the unknown?
why must we seek it?

Eastward again I laboured,
this time on foot, slowly, through dew-bright grass,
and saw the morning-glory untwist his white and purple.
Why must I watch this? why must I seek this cold beginning?
why must I know myself—alas, alas,—or try
to think I know myself? Here is that nescience,
that edge of clashing darkness, where I had birth.
Hence come my hand and heart. Hence comes the subtle thought
which, seeing chaos, knows itself, no more.
What comfort here? And if indeed this be
desire for first unconsciousness again;
if here, in daybreak's horror, I would drown;
if here in chaos I would sink my thought and drown;
were it not better, as the angel says,
to drown in sunset, having known the west?
Or is it better to have seen the east, before
we westward fly, with a westward dying world?
The morning-glory opened; the east was bright; the clouds
northward and southward parted before the sun;
the mountains brightened, east of Eden;
shafts of new light flew westward;
and westward I too returned, on lagging feet,
uncomforted, unthinking, sad, unseeing;
and felt my folded wings teased by the wind;
and homeward come in sadness, stood once more at the window;
marvelling at this great world which was myself.

XIX

Between the snow and summer, I heard Adam's anger
bitterly spoken, to Eve, and listened in secret, laughing,
while the spring fog was soft in the apple orchard.
And 'Woman,' he said, 'would you know nothing? would you be
ignorant all your days? dawdle here forever?
You saw our god go eastward—would you not go
eastward also, to see the things god saw?
Why, this is cowardice!' He glared at Eve;
but she smiled back with such impertinence,
that I was angry; although I knew her right.

'But what is eastward, Adam?' she said, laughing.
'Will we find there the rainbow's foot? or learn
why god is god? or why ourselves are mortal?
must we forever forage in the dark, with Eden
so close at hand? . . . Let us return to Eden!'

Then Adam took an oakbranch,
and broke it in his hands, in pride of strength;
and glared, and spoke again.

                        And 'Fool!' he said,
'what now is Eden? Eden was for our childhood.
Are we forever children? do we grow?
have you learned nothing, in this journey westward,
save that you want once more the fruits of Eden?
must you go back and play with acorns, grassblades, fernleaves?
Is nothing learned, with loss of innocence?
Eastward (I heard the gods say) lies that chaos
which groaned, and gave us birth. Are we such children, still,
that we must fear the darkness whence we come?'

'Eden is better,' said Eve. 'I want no chaos.'

'Would you remain a fool?'

                        'Why not?' said Eve.

'Ah, but you will not!' said Adam; 'for I will take you
eastward with me. There we will face the rock,
and learn the filthy roots that make us evil!
Come!'

        And he took her hand, and dragged her forth
a perilous journey (a mile or two) eastward, climbing
the hard hill, in the fog; and Eve protested
alarm, despair, and clung to him, and pleaded
and begged for Eden, and wept; but in her heart
laughed; for she knew how soon this work would end.

And I, who followed them, with soft and secret flight,
pitying both, and pleased with both, but angry also

that they should mimic thus so soon, unwitting,
the agonies of gods, waited, and watched;
knowing how soon fatigue would end this flight;
and knowing, too, that Eve knew; and that Adam,
after this show of courage, would relinquish
this splendid thirst for knowledge, and would sleep,

And thus it was. And when at last they rested,—
quarrelled and wept and slept,—I spread my wings
gladly above them; as an oak-tree might.

XX

Playing chess in the sunlight with the angel,
suddenly the angel's wing shadowed the pieces, curving
a sharp shadow forthright between the queen and bishop.
Then all was changed. That world of logic changed.
Eclipse was on me, a line of darkness dreadfully drawn;
and such a vision I had as sometimes comes in sleep.
Suppose—and this I thought, lifting upward
the shadowed bishop, so that his mitre was in the light—
suppose this board, in which all logic so clearly lies
in one bright plane, though now by shadow altered—
suppose this board, this game, had other dimensions?
If kings and queens had wings—

                              I moved my piece, pondered,
downward and upward into a world unguessed
by rooks and pawns; and said, more to myself
than to the angel, whose fingers lightly touched his king:
'If all were on one plane, how easy! If sorrow
were sorrow only for a single reason, not for
a thousand things! And if, for but a moment,
alas, for but a moment, we might know
the countless planes of feeling, or of knowledge, or of guess,
of which a moment's awareness is the intersection!
If we could see,—all in an instant,—
the lost flower, the tired hand, the slowed heartbeat, the cry
of water on rock, the sad history of the sand;
the tragedy of the half-remembered, the half-longed-for;

perceptions of time, of distance; self-distrust, self-praise;
simplicity of removal, and the wound it gives;
simplicity of approach, and the blessing it gives;
absence or presence of warmth, the come and go of light!
If we might know, at the instant itself of speech,
the atom's disaster in the blood, the new decision
made in the nerve-cell!'

               The angel moved his king,
stared through me, said: 'Why not go farther still?
what of the kidneys, the liver, the heart, the stomach?
Your speech is these: it is the sum, also, of these:
you are the sum of worlds within and worlds without.'
I took my knight by the ears, and lifted him,
and placed him in the sunlight, where he sparkled.
'Now I am changed,' I said; 'for by this action, surely,
I am a seedling's root that thrusts against a stone;
Eve with delight by Adam touched; the planet urging
his dying heat against the dying sun;
whispers returning, after touching the rock's face;
water returning, in a whisper, to the cloud.
And ah what hatreds, what furies, what deliriums,
moved to their end in this obliquity!
What loves, too, which the atom still remembers,
but I myself forget!'

               'And deaths,' the angel said.

XXI

It was when Lilith became an angel that I learned
(as before from Eve I guessed) how language too
leads one perforce into the south of worldmake.
She, with new wings, and vanity of wings,
preening her snow-plumes, smiling, fanning them slowly
for the new joy and power, lifting herself
a wing's width from the grass, and softly alighting
on winnowed flowers again, came to me, tempting.
Bringing her wings before her eyes, she smiled darkly,
hiding her face she laughed a little, and spoke
with such soft speech that I, distrusting, listened.

'Now that I have these wings which are my birthright,
these wings, of which Eve's innocence deprived me,
I shall again explore the world of darkness!
Come, god, and see how evil can flower in purple!
Come with me, I will teach you how the kiss
creates such kingdoms as your pure Adam never dreamed.'

Strange, too, the imaginations that she gave me
out of her voice and eyes, while, daylong and nightlong,
under the farthest nothing, we hung embraced.
One day and then another, with level flood of light,
far, far below us, poured the stars to westward;
and still we beat wide wings upon the ether;
and still I kissed the world-deep eyes and mouth.
Such wordless words she spoke as passed my knowledge:
said nothing, whispered, murmured, wept, caressed;
yet in my blood, and in my brain, began to build
fantastic worlds, and false too as fantastic.
Where the sun moved, and black as any cinder;
were the moon cleft, and blood poured down from it;
were darkness shed by stars, and in the darkness demons
swimming with wings of fire, their eyes like mouths;
and were I there, omnipotent in wonder,
now man, now woman, all alike pursuing,
and all alike embracing with swift wings,
drinking the darkness of innumerable mouths—

I trembled with the beginnings of this new power;
already half distinct I saw that fevered world;
inchoate lewdnesses becoming shapes,
shadows becoming lurid delicious lights,
all whirling, mad, and with delirium's wonder,
splendours of foulness. I withdrew my lips
from Lilith's lips, beat my right wing, and turned
to stare more soberly at this world of evil.

And so, my hand against her hair, I knew
how false this world, how true, and what its power;
and so, returning, brought its darkness back;
and built its splendid ramparts against Eden.

Blues for Ruby Matrix

I

Where's Ruby, where has she gone this evening?
what has her heart done, is it enlarged,
is she so flown with sombre magnificence,
is the web wrapped round her and she mad?
Why, she should have been here hours ago
and this a snowy night too and the soul starving—

Where's Ruby where has she gone today?
is she so glorious, is she so beautiful,
has she wings that thus abruptly she has gone?
come back Ruby, you are my light-of-love
(and her with a carbuncle too and no money)
where has she gone where has she gone?

I saw her once at a soda fountain,
you don't believe it you don't believe it do you?
I saw her once at a soda fountain
strangling sarsaparilla through a paper straw.
Where's Ruby gone where is she gone this evening—
incandescence has stopped, the night is dark.

I was a driver once and knew a thing or two,
the rails were right but everything else was wrong,
come back Ruby I will unwrap the web around you,
Oh I will blow the snow off your brain tonight
and polish your conscience for you and give you a tip
and show you the stairs to the bright door of hell.

Come Ruby, I will undo your rubber goloshes,
come Ruby, I will undo the clasps,
let us walk along the track of ice a little way
and talk a little way of ice and icicles

for you too knew the way the hoarfrost grew
on God's terrific wings—

how in the heart's horn comes the prince of pauses,
the peace between the agonies—O you
who found the stepping stone and brought it back,
gave it to me because I stood and loved you,
you who stood, when others stood no more,
on the abandoned and unprosperous shore.

Why it was you I loved and knew, and you
it was, the speechless and inalterable you
the one of the Aprils and the one of June,
O undiscoverable and unpursuable one
and one that was not one but two and three
or three that was not three but you and me.

Thus it comes, thus it comes Ruby,
woman who art not woman but a wound,
wound who art not wound but indeed a word,
word that art not word but truly a world
sprung spoken speaking spoiled and spent
in the brief darkness that the darkness meant.

                    II

But I was not convinced and said so too,
there among marigolds with Easter coming,
no I was not convinced had no convictions
and she was not convincing in the spring,
it was the wrong time, it was spring.

What I said was nobody's business, no,
nobody's business, I said the words straight out
and made no mention of the nightingale
nor of the willow buds or pines or palms
nor of the pleasure parks on Concy Isle
which Ikey Cohn decreed,

but I was blue and made no bones about it,
I was blue and said so to her face

there by the hot dog stand beneath the lamp
and not so far from the filling-station
I held her hand and told her face to face—

What did I tell her? Oh ask me something easy
why should I say the primrose has an eye,
why should I say the goldenrod is dusty
or the railroad long as hell from here to there,
why should I make remarks about her hair?

Tell me, brother, the little word to whisper,
tell me, brother, the little word to say,
tell me, sisters, the grand technique of love
or how to speak of beauty when you see it,
for what I said was angry that was all,
I told her to go to hell and well-damned stay there.

She made no mention of the nightingale,
why should she with no nightingales about,
nor of that other bird that burns to death.
The sidewalk was red brick beneath our feet,
the hot dog stand bright as the mouth of hell

but she was part and parcel of the brightness
that hell is said to have,
swallowed the night and smiled it back again,
laughed like a million lights, spoke like a cannon
she was a scenic railway crashing downward,
my straw hat blew away.

Pennies dimes nickels and quarters gone
and midnight come and the last boat so bright
so bright so light so cheap and full of people
all with their mouths and hands—Oh come and see
the world that lies behind the primrose eye
under the gilded teeth of Ikey Cohn—

come and see the water beside the ship,
see the white lincs of foam that cross the brain
and break against the skulltop and are bitter,

come and join us in the convincing spring
and learn how sad it is to stay out late.

Good-bye, Ruby, I am fed up with you,
good-bye Ruby, your nose needs powder,
I've got that midnight feeling in my heart,
I'll hate you till breakfast-time, till the poached eggs
make peace between us—

but you were behind the primrose eye and saw
the sunrise world and all the wings—and you
had known the ultimate and called it nothing
and you have sightseen God with tired eyes
and now come back to toast our daily bread.

III

What she had was something with no name,
if she were dead I'd carve it on a stone,
it was as right as rain as true as time,
necessary as rhythm in a tune,
what she had was only a word or two
spoken under the clock.

Delay was precious and we both delayed,
come on, Ruby, and hold on clock,
but there were springs unsprung or half-sprung, still
compelling mechanism to its stillness
and in the reading-room we read the word,
the silent word that silent spoke of meaning—

it was the now, it was the then, it was the when,
it was the snow, the rain, the wind,
the name and then the where, the name, the street,
the hearse, the cradle, the all-knowing judge—
and I unerring knew the pressing word
and she receptive knew it—

the midnight took my meaning, and the noon
engulfed it in broad sunlight, the swift cloud
carried it northward like a handkerchief

to lose it in the eventualness of time
while I with equal steps climbed up the stairs
away from the remembered, to descend—

and she ascending too, with equal steps,
and she descending too, before and after,
bearing the blossom, her angelic heart,
the thurible, the incense, her quick eyes
knowing the known and guessing the unknown
searching the shadow which my mind betrayed.

Why, we were here before, but now remember,
you at your time and I at mine,
both of us here to know this selfsame thing—
and now together know it, now together,
and in this pause together of the wings

touch the feathers, let the snow touch snow,
whisper recoil from whisper, frost shun frost,
that we may know what we have known already
but never with each other in this place,
or at this time, or even in this world,
and never with remembrance of before.

What she had was an evening paper, a purse,
a hat, a cape, and what I had was purpose,
but now, the purpose gone, I have—what have I Ruby,
if not a phrase of ice to carve on stone,
ambiguous skeleton of a whisper, gone
as soon as spoken, and myself alone?

IV

Boy, if I told you half of what I know—
the gulfs we cross by day to meet at night,
the Lincoln Highway and the Big Rock Candy Mountains,
the deserts of the Gulf of Mexico,
boy, if I told you how I spend my time
at night school learning all the stars of love

propound the constellations of her heart,
the North Star and the Southern Cross,
voyage to regions of the albatross
and come back spangled with bright frost of death—
boy, if you carved with me the curves I carve
against the dark undaunted ice of time

and knew those curves of hers that curve beyond
geometry of hand or eye or mind
into the bloodstream and above again,
westward under the sea with setting suns,
oblique dishonest and profound as hell,
corrupt, unchanging, changing, choice as steel—

Boy, if you went with me along her streets
under the windows of her lighted eyes,
saw the foul doors, the purlieus and the cats,
the filth put out the food received the money
the evil music grinning all its teeth,
cachinnations above the sauerkraut!

This is where she lives and loves, that Ruby,
this is where she lives and pays her way
among the unborn and the dead and dying,
the dirty and the sweating, pays her way
with sweat and guile and triumph and deceit
burning the empty paper bags and scraps.

Boy, if I told you where the money comes from
out of a silver mine in Colorado,
the unrefined refined and the bright goddess
brought all the way from chaos to Mike's Alley
and on her hand at noon to pay the rent
roof to prevent the rage of heaven's tent—

but if I told you half of what I know
I'd have to be the Gulf of Mexico
the Big Rock Candy Mountains in the spring
and every other big or little thing.

I'd wear the Milky Way out with my walking,
wear out my shoes with the walking blues.

Hush Ruby, I meant these words for someone else,
hush Ruby, it's all right now,
only a little student of geometry
who wanted to know the why and where of curves
went out and came back frozen by the stars
with geometric frostbite in his brain.

Take him in with you and warm him Ruby,
take him in with you, put him to sleep,
tell him the difference between truth and lying,
tell him where you've been and what you mean,
the clock, the closet, horror's cloaca too—
and wake him, when his heart is fed and dead.

v

But this was nothing boy, and I said nothing,
no leaf or love was born but it took time.
Come on and shake the cosmic dice, come seven,
come on and shake the bones for odd or even
but this was nothing and no one said a word.

I saw the palm leaf and I took it down, Ruby,
I saw the gold leaf and I took it down.
I saw the heaven leaf and I took it down, honey,
I saw the dead leaf and I took it down.

I saw the word that shaped the lips of water,
I saw the idea that shaped the mind of water,
I saw the thought of time that shaped the face,
I saw the face that brought disgrace to space.

But this was nothing, girl, and I said nothing,
nothing I thought, what could I think but nothing?
who nothing knew and was the seed of nothing,
the conscious No One watching Naught from Nowhere.

Take the palm leaf for what it is no other,
take the gold-leaf and put it down,
take the heaven-leaf and put it down, Ruby,
take the dead leaf and put it down—

for what is wisdom, wisdom is only this—
history of the world in a deathbed kiss,
past and to be in agony brought home,
and kingdom of darkness come.

VI

No use hanging round we must be going,
no use waiting before the evening altar
green screen of evening sky between paired stars
where the cloud worships and the wind is bowed,
there's no use waiting Ruby we must be moving.

You are a rock like that blue mountain too
jagged and scarred like that where the snow lingers
and I have seen the sunrise on white shoulders,
the orchid among the boulders,
the edelweiss and ewigkeit
and the retreating armies of the night.

No use waiting, Ruby, we will not hear,
the proud hosanna of the stars is not for us,
we will not hear them sing the silver word
nor see the angelic wings ascend between
the silver trumpets against a sky of icy green.

This we abandon, and though this have seen
see it no more, but take our evening down
along dark streets that you have made your own,
the wretched streets that in-and-out are you,
there where the cry of pain is in the bone

and where your darkness prowls around us nightlong,
approaches and retreats, confronts us snarling,
devours the hours—is this your house Ruby,
are these your stairs, is that your window open,
is there a bed a ceiling above the bed?

do voices come and go and slam of doors?
Smells of fecundity, the human spawn,
far off the cries of trains, the taxi's ticking

217

is all coincidence that thus together
everything meets upon this tip of time—

your hand that murdered men or drew the morning
out of the seventh vial, or rolled the mountains
against the tombs of all the gods, or poured
the zeros one on other and destroyed
the indestructible to create the new—

came like a flame from sand, reentered water,
was braided like the ice, became a wall
sang through the trumpet of eternity
and now, descended, holds a greasy key
and presses it against a greasy lock—

Farewell Ruby, for this is where I leave you
your hand releases me its filth is on me,
the holy filth of long corruption comes
coldly upon me as an absolution,
sharply we flower in this foul farewell.

VII

But God's terrific wing that day came down,
loud on the world as loud and white as snow
out of the blue the white and then the silence.
O Ruby, come again and turn the time.

Ruby, your name is matrix, rock of ages
cloven by lightning, smitten by thunder,
the surged upon deep shore interminable,
the long, the nebulous waves, the foam of time,

beating upon you, breaking upon you foaming,
the worldlong fruitfulness of assuaging sea,
hammers of foam, O Ruby come again
be broken for our simple coming forth—

let the rocks fall upon us with fearful sound,
the long bright glacier of the stars be broken,

the beginning and the final word be spoken,
come again, come again, and turn the world.

This world that is your turning and returning,
matrix mother mistress menstrual moon,
wafer of scarlet in the virgin void,
O come again and turn the world to thought.

But God's terrific wing that day came down
snow on the world, and Ruby you were snow,
deceitful whiteness and the blood concealed
so that the world might know how worlds will end.

The Kid

PROEM

WILLIAM BLACKSTONE (Died 1675)

Where now he roves, by wood or swamp whatever,
the always restless, always moving on,
his books burned, and his own book lost forever,
under the cold stars of New England, gone,

scholar who loved, and therefor left, the most,
secret and solitary, no Indian-giver,
who to his own cost played the generous host
and asked adventurers across his river:

what would he make of us, if he could see,
after so many tides have ringed this coast,
what manner of men his children's children be
to welcome home his still inquisitive ghost?

He, more than all, of individual grace,
the pilgrim innocence, self-knowledge sure,

stepped like an angel in this savage place,
and, in all nature, found no evil-doer.

A summer's freedom on a bramble shore
whose wild rose the Lords Bishop could not blight,
then the Lords Brethren saw him close his door,
bidding his orchards, and his house, good-night.

Now by the lamplit wall his friendly nod
salutes the late wayfarer on that hill
where wych-elms ward some semblance of the sod
he knew by Cam's side, and he measures still

the common field he found and kept aright,
setting his rose-trees and his fruit-trees out:
these, and his books, and truth, all his delight,
and the locked heart of man his only doubt.

I. THE WITNESS

Who saw the Kid when he rose from the east
riding the bridled and fire-bright Beast?
heard him shout from the surf-gold, streaming
crupper and bit, the surcingle gleaming,
elbows sharp against daybreak sky,
the reins held light and the hands held high?
The clouds above him and the breakers below
blazed with glory, and the Kid also.
Who saw that hero, that pinto, come
like one indivisible Word from foam?

    The horseshoe crab and the nighthawk did,
    the quawk and the tern and the chickadee did,
    yes, and the little green grasshopper did,
    they saw the Kid, they heard the Kid.

Who heard that lad leap down from a cloud,
over the night hard hoofbeats pounding,
rapid and far or softer sounding,

nearer thudding, then sudden and loud?
The stars rode down, their hooves were bright:
they threshed the morning to sheaves of light.
Who heard from heaven that ghost tattoo,
down hyaline stairs of quartz and blue,
and then *yippee—yippee—halloo?*

The bullbriar patch and the groundhog did,
the Indian boy in the birch-tree hid,
the solemn cricket and the fat katydid,
these were the ones who saw the Kid.

To Old Mar River from hoarse Monomoy
they eyed that pony, they admired that boy,
watched him skim over billows of oak
up before sunup and away like smoke.
He sped to the river, and they saw him span
wide water as only a rainbow can,
down the long valley a sun-ghost flinging,
lariat's whistle and a noose of singing.

The catfish slick and the cunning 'possum,
the hummingbird moth in the scuppernong blossom,
the moccasin's braid in the bog-hole hid,
they heard the Kid, they knew the Kid.

And these too knew him: a lynx of stone.
Rats' eyes, pricked in the blue of the moon.
Frogs' eyes, blinking like bubbles in ooze,
bedded by the creek in twos and twos.
The doe, turned tail, and the buck at stand,
shadows and eyes in the innocent land:
snuffings and shadows, the lone wolf howl,
and far in the Ozarks the quaver of an owl.

And westward, seaward, he drew the horizon,
following the Sioux, who followed the bison,
westward, along the Missouri no more,
far back remembered like Ohio's shore,
far back forgotten like the moosewood tree

and dust in the mouth on a prairie sea,
the watergap crossed, the chinquapins gone,
breast-high laurel, and still heading on.

I'm away, I'm away, I'm away to the west,
I'll stay no more on my mother's breast,
my sister can study the golden rule,
my little brothers can traipse to school
my pa he can curse, my ma she can cry,
they'll all forgive me in the sweet by-and-by,
I come from heaven and to heaven I'll go,
but what's in between I'm a-wantin' to know!

Who picked up the words from the prophet's mouth?
Grizzly in the north, and longhorn south.
Who bore witness to that faring-forth?
Buzzard in the south, and eagle in the north.
Prairie-dog cities swarming in the sun,
golden in the evening, and then not one.
Buffalo spine. A high grass growing.
Rattlesnake rattle and tumbleweed blowing.

And these too witnessed: the sachem's daughter,
crouched by the creek for a pitcher of water:
riding like the wind—she cried as she ran—
that was no horse, and that was no man.
Forked from his fist came the lightning stroke,
the double thunder and a puff of smoke:
the double thunder and the lightning twice,
his hair like fire and his eyes like ice;
and a pinto pony, a wing of flame,
whinnying and gone as quick as it came.

The rain-god, sure! The little cloud rose
up the dark mountain and over pale snows,
thunder whizzed down from an eyried shelf,
and lo, the bright bird on the peak itself.
A flash through sunset, a meteor falling,
halloos and echoes in hollow rock calling,
halloos and echoes all night till dawn,
night stiff with rain, but the rain-god gone.

Who watched that spirit shoot down to the west,
sun going home to the sun-god's breast?
or praised that triumph, that last homecoming,
the pride, the glory, and the end of roaming?
The farewell darkness of night to love him,
a rainbow of stars for a crown above him,
who saw that pinto, that hero, go,
to the world forever, the world below?

> The old sequoia and the sea-hawk did,
> the barnacled lion in his sea-cave hid,
> the sand and the surge and the sea-fog did,
> they hailed the Kid, farewelled the Kid.

And these too hailed him: the high sierra:
desert, and rock, and the cordillera:
a glacier's leavings, a god's moraine,
a tower of ice, and a wall of rain.
They caught his hymn as it fell to the sea
from condor's shadow and sugarpine-tree:
of might in singleness, a crown in fate,
the everlasting of the golden gate.

II. THE LAND

The sun-cymbal strikes: and a land of voices
begins, and from ocean to ocean rejoices:
whispers of laughter: wave making mock
in glittering derision of water on rock:
the waterfall seethes: the pine-barren breathes:
cloud over watershed steams and wreathes:
fog slips down to drip into rain,
the cataract's secret loose on the plain:
grassland, swampland, the everglade sighing,
sighing in the rank sun, fetlocks drying.

And rivers: rivers with their proud hosanna:
Chattahoochee: Tallahassee: Susquehanna
Savannah, high-yaller, and Arkansas, red:

Colorado bowling in a mile-deep bed:
Hendrik Hudson, with snow on his breast,
and Great Meridian that walls off the west.
What malice to rustle? what love-talk babbling?
Pebbles in a pool, and a freshet gabbling.
Drip-drop tinkle, an icicled fern,
honing of a rock, a bouldered churn,
and downward, sliding, with cliff-high roar,
merryflashed wave past a vanishing shore.
Who's there? who's here? The palmetto rattles.
The slow moss hisses. The cottonwood tattles.

Listen: the wind from the prairie is blowing:
listen: the harp-string whisper of snowing:
avalanche mutter: the granite scraped bare:
horny-cry of ice on the rime-bright air.
What leaves, what grasses, what reeds, what flowers?
Sun over cloud cliff, cloud over showers.
And eastward, quartering, countering the sun,
a maze of lazy voices buzzing all as one.
River-mud slumping in a red lump, gone:
snag at the riverbend, blanched like bone:
moon-scented sweetgrass, a land unplowed:
whirled over sumach, the grasshopper cloud.

What sticks? what stones? what cavern? what briar?
Crag for the bighorn and the eagle's gyre.
The heat-song singing, the sun gone down,
and timberwolf hymn from the butte to the moon:
star for the firefly, stem for the thrush,
a fox on the sidehill, a bird in the bush.
South roar the rivers: east roars the weather:
all sounds gather in a vast wave together:
beast cry and bird song, a multitude of voices,
where, between oceans, the long land rejoices.
Leaf-step, rain-step: the canebrake rattles:
fog-step, dew-step: the silverleaf tattles.

III. THE FIRST VISION

Here, to be first, is not to find:
here, to be first, is the first mind.
Here, to be first, is not to claim,
but to give lonely truth a name.

He moved to the north, moved to the south,   William
camped on sand at the river's mouth,   Blackstone
camped in the sun, woke in the rain,
then struck his camp and moved it again.
Sticks for a fire, the fire put out,
fox-bark too close, or the owlet's shout:
a leaf displaced, the Observers near,
a secret company, but not to fear.
Stealth under stars, and stars to be read,
lying on his back, the Book overhead—
the Plow, the Pole, but positions strange,
direction altered, and a vaster range.
Who's there? who's here? The shades but shifted.
Eyes under leaves, and an oak-bough lifted.
Water-song, reed-song: and strange birds, too,
none, save one, with a voice he knew.
Was God's path here? By what to be known?
What trail, what blaze, in the wilderness shown?
Bullbriar, hacked for a snake-green lair:
snow on the leafmold, exceeding fair:
such to be studied, and for such, a prayer.
Morning and evening, Lord, I beseech Thee,
suffer my cry from this woode to reach Thee,
these are Thy presents, Thy heart I find
in the dark forest in sleet and winde.
As on the sea Thou sailedst before,
a cloud, that our shippe might see this shore,
so now Thou walkest, these trees Thy feet,
and in this brooke Thy heart doth beat.
Lorde, I am fearless, Thy mercy shown,
for where Thou art there is nought unknown:
what are these seemings save Thine own?

O grant Thy servant his grace of dayes
whose hours shall all be filled with praise:
here Thy newe workes must numb'red be
and fair names fitted to beast and tree.
All to be learned, all to be loved,
thus ever freshe Thy kingdom proved.

He moved to the north: by the harbor found
a sweet spring bubbling in open ground:
on a clear hill, by an oystred river,
and here, he thought, I shall dwell forever.
A plat of roses, a plot of trees,
apples, pears, and a skep of bees,
friends in the village, true Indian friends,
here Lord in joye my journey ends.
What should I want but bookes on shelf—
these few I have—and that dark selfe
that poures within me, a chartless sea,
where every landfall is named for Thee?
What other voyage could solace me?
Thou being pilot, Lord, I find
untrodden kingdoms in the minde:
freedom is all my coin: and these
humilities and simplicities,
Thy humblest creatures, birds and flowers,
instruct and ornament my hours.

. . . But the Lords Brethren came, and then
Lords Bishop also: the world of men
crossed his river. He moved again,
southward, a last time closed his door:
then to the wilderness once more.
Loud, loud, the savage sun: the sky
bright with pigeons: the jackal's cry
echoed the loon; and wolves, at night,
howled to the moon. But mind's delight
embracing these and all, he moved
deliberate in a world he loved.
Angelick pengwins trod that shore:
fearless he heard the lyon's roar:
pale honeysuckle ringed the page,

where, in a noon, he read an age.
What rills? what meads? what mast? what flowers,
to be inscribed in a Book of Hours?
What meditation, song, and prayer,
heard on the air and copied fair?
And love's green margin everywhere.
But house and book are burned and lost,
and death is one more river crossed:
shadow and voice together gone,
westward, southward, the ghost moves on.

IV. SECOND VISION:
THE AMBIGUITY

In secret wood, where once he stood,
hard by the banks of lacrym flood,
two sister voices soft he heard
dividing world in flesh and word:
as if two angels in his soul
leaned in debate from pole to pole:
argument, as of night and day,
whether 'twere wise to go or stay.
Sometimes the voices were as one,
then again broke that unison.
Both to be free they were agreed,
but challenged whose the greater need.
Was freedom of the heart? or hand?
of secret soul? or the wide land?
And were it better to stir or stand?
Thenceforth the traveler was possessed
by the two sibyls in his breast:
under the wood, beside the stream,
the changing voices shaped his dream.
Sometimes, to soothe that discontent,
to the soul's underworld he went,
cried his O Altitudo there,
but with the accents of despair:
for doubts and shades stood everywhere.
Was freedom but to be masterless?
not to be found in wilderness?

Anne
Bradstreet

And then, which wilderness were best,
that of the world, or of the breast?
Sometimes in stillness the voice sings,
but loudly too when the broadaxe rings.
Shadow and voice together gone,
inward, outward, the ghost moves on.

V. THE MARTYRDOM

He turned on his tracks: to the puritans came:
bore witness to bigots, was martyred in shame:
no church found for truths, and no house for faith,
but choir of the word, and the walls of breath:
an arbor of saplings, a shanty of wood,
for winter's whistlings, a river in flood.
This season, how grievous, how bitter this coast,   *Lawrence,*
where love finds no chapel, no comfort a ghost!   *Cassandra,*
Clap wings and begone, no lantern hangs here,   *Daniel,*
but hatred and darkness, the dead of the year.   *Josiah,*
Cry, cry, for New England, New Canaan indeed!   *and*
Dear ghosts of this forest, who suffer and bleed,   *Provided*
your names shall be chalice, your voices cry still,   *Southwick*
who were whipped at a cart's-tail and hanged on a hill.
Lashed at a cart's-tail, through three towns driven,
hanged on a hill by the servants of heaven,
banished, or perished, or sold as a slave,
poor body unhouseled, a hole for a grave—
cry, cry for New England! The true voices speak,
while granites of Norton and Endicott break.
This is my bodye: let it be my truth:
tear it in pieces, if ye have not ruth:
freely I give it, let it die, let it rot:
but as for your sentence, I matter it not.
Well know you the things we said in this place:
the enlargement of God we find in His grace:
come now what His wisdom and pleasure approve,
our rest and our life in His infinite love.
By the wills of men captive: made free by the Son:
chapter eight, in the Gospel according to John.

VI. THE KID

He turned to the land: forgot his name: Hector
changing and changeless went and came: St. John de
dreamed blood-knowledge as he slept in nature: Crèvecoeur
sucked blood-knowledge from the blood of the creature:
wing-thrust learned in the terror on face:
heartbeat probed in the heartbeat's place:
knew hummingbird fury: the hoof-hole still
clear under water, which sand would fill:
tension and torsion, snakes on the ground,
a mortal agony in combat bound:
tore leaves, broke ferns, for a word on the tongue: John
persimmon plucked for a new song sung: James
preached, as he killed: lived in a lair: Audubon
ate musquash, moosemeat, the fat of the bear:
spoke to his own soul, spoke to the stream, Henry
Lord, lend me wisdom, Lord, let me dream: David
spent in thy heart was this sunshine day,   Thoreau
now in the evening a flute I'll play,
a flute in the forest, these pages to read,
a fly on the goldenrod, no more I'll need.
He trucked with the Indians: laid axe to root: John
packed his knapsack with the seed of fruit: Chapman
appleseed flung like flame in a wood:
fished pond and river, trod eels from mud;
framed a corncrib, and plowed up a field,
planted his corn and brought it to yield:
quit that clearing and a cabin of logs,
traded his store-goods and bought him some hogs;
and then, once more with an itching foot,
lashed a new raft, laying axe to root,
farewelled his folks, and floated down river,
to be home in the spring or else gone forever.

Said Tidewater Johnny to Bluewater Johnny,
you got to go west if you want to make money,
we built up the cities and filled them with people,

piled up a church and on top put a steeple,
and the cities are pretty, but the forest is best,
if you want to be private you got to go west.
Said Buckskin Johnny to Canebrake Johnny,
you got to climb trees if you want to eat honey,
the streets are well cobbled, the coaches are fine,
the ladies wear satin, the taverns have wine,
new immigrants skip from the packets each day,
set foot on the jetty, then up and away,
and the cities are pretty, but the prairie is best,
no money we'll need if we go to the west.
Said Catskill Johnny to Swannikan Johnny,
you fetch a horse and I'll find a pony,
we'll hitch Conestoga to a comet's tail
and hurry out west on the wilderness trail.
Nice manners and music are all very well,
and a college is fit for the son of a swell,
let moneybags tot up his slaves and his rum,
we're off to a place where a man has more room.
Go twing, go twang, go twang your guitar,
we'll roll all night to the prairie star,
there's no more Indians to fight, move on
where the Boone and Blackstone ghosts are gone:
you live but once, you're a long time dead—
who but a fool wants to die in bed?
And as for women, why, love 'em and leave 'em,
you got to love 'em but you got to grieve 'em.
Go twing your guitar, go twing, go twang,
I'm away to the coast on a wild mustang,
you need no ticket for the Golden Gate,
and the Big Rock Candy Mountains wait:
I've heard of a town named Snake-Eye Sue
with a bank and a bar and a damned fine view,
fourteen houses made of old tin cans,
but let me tell you that town is a man's:
that town is a man's, that's what they say,
and my name is the Kid, and I'm on my way!

Westward he rode, and the masks he wore:
southward he rode, and the names he bore.
Roared into town like a railroad train,

notched his gun, then notched it again.
He called his home the enchanted mesa:
came like a rustler, went like a greaser:
was twenty times shot and thirty times hung,
forty times captured and fifty times sprung:
ate mush and molasses with a long-handled spoon,
danced a square-dance from midnight to noon,
swing your partners, and now sashay,
do-se-do, give the gals away,
the promenade, and the allemande,
and pickin' posies on the Rio Grande:
kissed all the gals, and never missed one,
then rode out of town like a son-of-a-gun.
An old panhandler with the face of a moose *Kit*
said, Chew terbaccer and swaller the juice, *Carson*
I seen him with my own eyes, I did,
and I'm a horsethief if it wasn't the Kid.
Sandy and short, and his eyes was blue,
and what he looked at he looked right through.
A bindlestiff by the name of Joe
swore up and down it couldn't be so:
No sir, you ain't got the facts at all,
he wasn't freckled, and he wasn't small,
his name was Christopher, it wasn't Kit,
and he rode a pinto without no bit.
Said Bad Land Ike: It can't be the same. *Billy*
I saw him in Pecos when he jumped my claim. *the*
If a coffin nail's dead, then the Kid is dead. *Kid*
His eyes were blue but his blood was red,
and they covered him up with an old bedspread.
No chick, no child, and no woman had he,
and they buried his body by a buckeye tree.

Rain-song and sun-song: rain from the sea:
here is my body, my truth let it be:
rain from the east and rain from the west
my body asleep in the deep earth's breast:
carve the stone tree, carve the stone urn,
the hourglass carve that never will turn,
the death's-head grinning, the willow-tree weeping,
my body asleep, and the raindrop dripping.

Stones! stones! stones!—and westward they face:
but thousands of miles have I been from this place:
thousands of waters my forefoot found,
in thousands of meadows my plow broke ground.
Here is my truth, and the page I turned:
but there, too, truth, and the wage I earned:
and the wisdom, also, that in rage I learned.
I drove the nails in the house I built: *Paul*
hammered a swordblade, and carved a hilt: *Revere*
blew the fine glass, poured lead in a mold,
and figured a ewer in pewter and gold:
for secret study, in sun and in shade,   *Benjamin*
I cast my type and my own book made,   *Franklin*
in subtler substance than silver wrought
the nerve of vision and the pulse of thought:
the verse of the hand, the verse of the eye,
the verse of the clear soul under the sky.
Stranger, as you are, so once was I.

What fiddles, what prayers, what dirge, what cry?
Skull in the desert and sand under sky.
Hands of cactus, and buffalo bones,
and a tassel of pine on a cairn of stones.
In the tall timber the true axe rings
where the ox draws wood and the woodsman sings:
a mountain of gold down the river is poured,
and a poppy's in bloom in praise of the Lord.
The praise is said, the prayer is done,
the fiddles are broken, but the ghost moves on.

VII. THE AWAKENING

Dark was the forest, dark was the mind:
dark the trail that he stooped to find:
dark, dark, dark, in the midnight lost,
in self's own midnight, the seeking ghost.
Listen to the tree, press leaves apart:
listen to the blood, the evergreen heart:
deep, deep, deep, the water in the soul,

there will I baptize, and there be whole.
Dark, dark, dark, in this knowledge immersed,
by filth, by fire, and by frost aspersed,
in horror, in terror, in the depths of sleep,
I shudder, I grow, and my roots are deep.
The leaf is spoken: the granite is said:
now I am born, for the king is dead:
now I awake, for the father is dead.
Dark is the forest when false dawn looms—
darkest now, when the true day comes.
Now I am waking: now I begin:
writhe like a snake from the outworn skin:
and I open my eyes: and the world looks in!

VII. THE LAST VISION

Said Railway Willy, O carry me back
on the golden engine and the silver track,
carry back east in a tall caboose
this broken-down body that's no more use.
I ain't seen Susie for sixteen years,
and the cinders are in my hair and ears,
I laid my rail and I drove my spike,
but the sound of the whistle is what I like:
all night I wait till I hear that freight,
and I set my watch, for it's never late.
We tunneled the mountain, we bridged the river,
we split the Rockies and they're split forever,
we coasted down to Pacific foam,
but now I'm dying and I want to go home.
Buffalo Gal, won't you come out tonight?
I'm headed east, and the signal's right.

O I'm headed for home, said Steamboat Bill
on the Old Big River that shines uphill,
headed for the north from New Orleans,
feeding my fires on pork and beans.
I'll bowl through the chutes on the morning dew
and blow my whistle like I used to do,
blow my whistle and bowl through the chutes,

up from the bayous and away to the buttes.
O larboard leadsman, with your cry 'half twain!'
O Arkansas Traveler, with your rod and chain!
git aboard, it's time to go east again.
They've finished the cities, they're pretty to see,
and they're waiting to greet us with a golden key.

South poured the rivers: east went the dream:
east flew the glitter like a cloud of steam:
east coiled the dream like a wraith of smoke
on fields of clover that were forests of oak:
snow-song hovering, bird-song heard,
deep underground the shudder of the word:
death-knowledge whispered, death-knowledge guessed,
farewell the sunset, farewell the west:
rise up so early in the morn, my heart,
the road turns east and it's time to start:
rise up so early in the morn, my soul·
the roadstead's ready and the heart is whole.

He changed his name: Ahab became:
Ahab, and Ishmael, but the Kid just the same: *Herman*
his father's gods in a fury forswore   *Melville*
for a god more evil, but to worship more:
the god of hatred, of bland white evil,
the world incarnate as a blind white devil:
hurricane's wing: the capricious rage
that spares the pollen on the printed page
and then in frolic lays waste an age.
From the west returning, and the axe let be,
he turned, returning, to his mother, the sea:
islands, the foreshore, a gale in the Sound,
packets and whalers to the far east bound:
the full-moon tide, and the twin isles blest,
where Coffin and Daggett in God's Acre rest:
John and Lydia, that lovely payre,
a whale killed him, her body lyes here.

What thoughts? what hymns? what prayers? what altar?
Words out of tempest, and footsteps falter.
The sea-dark sounded, the dread descent

to fathom's meaning, a depth unmeant:
eyes to the self's black sea-heart turned,
the fouled line followed, the labyrinth learned.
Was God's path here? By what to be known?
What false channel-mark in the whale-path shown?
In Gulf Stream soul, or maelstrom heart,
what vortex to quarter, what shoals to chart?
Morning and evening, Lord, I reject Thee.
In fraud and fury, as in fire, I detect Thee.
In lust and in death I take and forsake Thee.
In breath and corruption I make Thee and break Thee.
In hate and despair I find Thee and lose Thee.
In breeding and bleeding I refuse Thee and use Thee.
In purposed or aimless I name Thee and shame Thee.
Wait Thou unknown, I'll seek Thee and claim Thee!

He plunged to the center, and found it vast.   Willard
Soared to the future, and found it past.   Gibbs
Always escaping the claws of clause,
inward or outward, the Laws and Cause:
mask under mask, face behind face,
name within name, place beneath place.
Ring within ring, he uncovered his pain:
found light in darkness, then darkness again: Henry
world whorled in world the whorl of his thought,   Adams
shape under series the godhead he sought:
for orbit's ritual and atom's cry   Brooks
he shot down the soul, saw it fall from the sky,   Adams
the invisible sighted, invisibly slain,
and darkly, in blood, resurrected again.
Working and weeping, Lord, I defy Thee.
In hurt and injustice I know and deny Thee.
Asleep in my slumber, I shake Thee and wake Thee,
in image, or number, or dream, to remake Thee.
Come terror, come horror, no need to escape Thee:
dipped in my death, I receive Thee and shape Thee!

Free flew the ghost: from the blood, from the land!   Walt
Hymned with the sea-voice on Paumanok sand!   Whitman
Broke like a billow, skimmed like a bird,

a rainbow on Greylock, by Walden a word!
And sleeps in the churchyard, unlaureled the stone,   *Emily*
where lies the intrinsic, unknown, and alone.   *Dickinson*

Mayflower

Listen: the ancient voices hail us from the farther shore:
now, more than ever, in the New England spring,
we hear from the sea once more
the ghostly leave-takings, the hawser falling, the anchor weighing,
cries and farewells, the weeping on the quayside, and the praying:
and the devout fathers, with no thought to fail,
westward to unknown waters set joyless sail,
and at length, 'by God's providence,' 'by break of day espied
land, which we deemed to be Cape Cod.'
'It caused us to rejoice together and praise God,
seeing so goodly a land, and wooded to the brink of the sea.'
And still we share that providential tide,
the pleasant bay, wooded on every side
with 'oaks, pines, juniper, sassafras,' and the wild fowl rising
in clouds and numbers past surmising.
Yes: the ancient voices speak once more,
as spring, praised then by Will and Ben,
winds up our country clock again:
their spring, still living, now
when caterpillars tent the bough,
and seagulls speak
over the ale-wives running in Payne Creek.
The lyre-tree, seven-branched, the ancient plum, has cast
her sterile bloom, and the soft skin is cast
to glisten on the broken wall,
where the new snake sleeps in altered light;
and before sun-up, and late at night,
the pinkwinks shrill, the pinkwinks trill,
crying from the bog's edge to lost Sheepfold Hill.

236

Spring, spring, spring, spring, they cry,
water voice and reed voice,
spring, spring, spring, spring, they rejoice,
we who never die, never die!
But already the mayflower on the side hill is brown and dry,
Dry Hill is dry, the bog is drained,
and although for weeks it has not rained,
and the quick plough breaks dust,
yet towards summer the golden-rod and wormwood thrust.
The woodchuck is in the peas. And on his log,
the whip-poor-will shrieks and thumps in the bright May-morning
     fog.

Three hundred years from Will and Ben,
and the crab-apple sage at Hawthornden;
and now they wind our country clock again,
themselves, whose will it was that wound it then.
Three hundred years of snow and change,
the Mermaid voices growing lost and strange;
heard at first clearly on this yellow sand,
ghost voices, shadow of ghost and whisper of ghost,
haunting us briefly in the bright and savage land,
heard in the sea-roar, then sunk in silence, lost.
Yet not lost wholly:
in deed, in charter, and in covenant sweetly kept,
in laws and ordinances, in the Quaker's Thee and Thou,
in the grave rites of birth and death, the marriage vow,
and the ballad's melancholy.
Sung by the driftwood fire or behind the plough,
in the summer-kitchen to the warm cricket-song,
sung at maying, sung at haying,
shouted at husking to the fiddle's playing,
murmured to the cradle's rocking,
and the wheel humming, the treadle knocking.
And in the names kept too: sorrel and purslane,
ground-ivy; catnip, elecampane,
burdock and spurge, and sultry tansy,
woad-waxen, and the johnny-jump-up pansy.
Yet even so, though in the observance kept,
here most of all where first our fathers stept,
was something of the spirit that became idle, and at last

lost all that love; and heard no more
the voices singing from a distant shore.
Intricately, into the present, sank the past:
or, dreaming only of the future, slept.

II

God's Acres once were plenty, the harvest good:
five churchyards, six, in this sparse neighbourhood,
each with its huddled parish of straight stones,
green rows of sod above neat rows of bones.
The weeping willow grieves above the urn,
the hour-glass with wings awaits its immortal turn:
on every slab a story and a glory,
the death's head grinning his *memento mori*.
All face the sunset, too: all face the west.
What dream was this of a more perfect rest—?
One would have thought the east, that the first ray
might touch them out of darkness into day.
Or were they sceptics, and perforce, in doubt,
wistful to watch the last of light go out?
And in the sunset the names look westward, names like eyes:
the sweet-sounding and still watchful names. Here lies
Mercy or Thankful, here Amanda Clark,
the wife of Rufus; nor do they dread the dark,
but gaily now step down the road past Stony Brook,
call from the pasture as from the pages of a book,
their own book, by their own lives written,
each look and laugh and heartache, nothing forgotten.
Rufus it was who cleared of bullbriar the Long Field,
walled it with fieldstone, and brought to fabulous yield
the clay-damp corner plot, where wild grape twines.
Amanda planted the cedars, the trumpet-vines,
mint-beds, and matrimony vine, and columbines.
Each child set out and tended his own tree,
to each his name was given. Thus, they still live, still see:
Mercy, Deborah, Thankful, Rufus and Amanda Clark,
trees that praise sunlight, voices that praise the dark.
The houses are gone, the little shops are gone,
squirrels preach in the chapel. A row of stone
all now that's left of the cobbler's, or in tall grass

a scrap of harness where once the tannery was.
And the blue lilacs, the grey laylocks, take possession
round every haunted cellar-hole, like an obsession:
keep watch in the dead houses, on vanished stairs,
where Ephraim or Ahira mended chairs:
sneak up the slope where once the smoke-house stood
and herrings bronzed in smoke of sweet fernwood.
Lost, lost, lost, lost—the bells from Quivett Neck
sing through the Sabbath fog over ruin and wreck,
roofs sinking, walls falling, ploughland grown up to wood.
Five churchyards, six, in this sparse neighbourhood:
God's Acres once were plenty, the harvest good.

III

Three hundred years: in time's eye only a moment.
Time only for the catbird's wail,
from one June to another, flaunting his tail,
the joyful celebrant with his own mournful comment.
Time only for the single dream,
as, in this misty morning, all our generations seem,
seem only one, one face, one hope, one name:
those who first crossed the sea, first came,
and the newborn grandchild, crying, one and the same.
Yes now, now most of all, in the fateful glare
of mankind's hatred everywhere,
time yields its place, with its own bell
uncharms and then recharms its spell:
and time is gone, but everything else is here,
all is clear, all is one day, one year,
the many generations seem,
and are, one single purpose, one single name and dream.
Three hundred years from Will and Ben
our country clock's wound up again.
And as it chimes we hear ourselves still saying
the living words which they said then—
words for haying, words for maying,
love of earth, love of love, love of God,
but most the strong-rooted and sweet-smelling love of sod,
earth natural and native in the clay-red heart,
ourselves like pines in the sand growing, part

of the deep water underground,
the wild rose in the mouth, the sound
of leaves in surf and surf in leaves,
wind suffering in the chimney and round the eaves,
forgetfulness in the chattering brook, sleepiness in the sand,
forget-me-nots in the eyes, moonlight in the palm of the hand.

All's here, all's kept, for now
spring brings back the selfsame apple bough
that braved the sea three hundred years ago.
It is our heart, our love, which we had lost,
our very ghost,
forgotten in trouble on an alien coast.
Now, in the many-voiced country lane
which parts the fields of poverty grass and clover,
as the loud quail repeats twice over
Bob White, not quite, not quite, Bob White,
see it again and say it again,
world without end to love and have it,
bee-blossom heart to love and live it,
this holy land, our faith itself, to share again
with our godfathers, Will and Ben.

Hallowe'en

I

All Saints', All Hallows',
All Souls', and Hallowe'en,
which is the evening of the last of October,
and the harvest moon full:
and the first of November, Allerheiligen,
and the second of November, Allerseelen.
The moon, dead brother, lights her bonfire
behind Sheepfold Hill, old corpse-fire
blazing through the oaktrees, the bone-fire
which, in the forests, the priests called *ignis ossium.*

And again you come to complain and to haunt me,
you and the others, the homeless: the bells
trill in the twilight, held by no fingers,
touched by no hand of the living, the voices
under the bronze cloud circle the bonfire,
wing-voice and bat-voice and tree-voice:
and the spotted pebble, flung hissing in flames,
is lost in the ashes, and with it your soul.
It is you at the fire's edge, grandfather—!
your skeleton dancing, the pumpkin-head glaring,
the corpse-light through the pierced eyes and slashed mouth,
you, past the gas-works and the power-plant drifting,
and the old car-tracks and the railroad crossing,
but not, no, not again to the Heath of Simmering
where you watched little rafts of gay candles
floating like fireflies down the Danube, the souls
of those who had drowned in the river! There you
with alien eyes saw the ancient god, there heard
with alien ears the *Allerseelen, Allerheiligen*,
the candles on grave-mounds, and the flowers,
the procession of the living with wreaths
to the hillside cemeteries in the mountains,
and, after dark, the processions of the dead
to the lost threshold, the lost hearthstone.
And now you come back to complain and to haunt me,
you, and my brother, and the others.
Was your vision of god not enough, that you come
for the vision of the not-yet-dead, and the cricket's
chirp on the still-warm hearthstone?

II

In the old time, the old country,
these two days, these two holy days,
were devoted to the dead. At the end of summer,
in the first haze of autumn stolen in from the sea,
at Samhain, the end of summer,
salt smell of kelp mixed with scent of the windfall
and whirled up the chalk path at daybreak,
we sacrificed a white horse to the sun-god
and kindled great fires on the hills

and nightlong we danced in circles
with straw-plaits blazing on pitchforks.
We sacrificed too to the moon-god,
an effigy, a simulacrum,
on this night, Hallowe'en, for we knew
the spirits of the dead were released, and would come
to rattle our latches and sit at the table. At Vespers,
in the dank churchyard, in the ossuary,
where the bones from an over-full graveyard were crammed,
we went in and knelt among bones. And the bones
(wing-voice and tree-voice and wind-voice)
suddenly were singing about us
joined in complaint and besought us
for prayers and more prayers, while the candles
flickered in the draft on grave-mounds.
Then on clean cloth we laid out the supper,
the hot pancakes, and the curds, and the cider,
and banked well the fire, and set the chairs round it,
said a prayer, and to bed.

In the old time, the old country:
but now none remembers, now they become
the forgotten, the lost and forgotten. O lost and forgotten,
you homeless and hearthless, you maskers and dancers,
masquerading as witches, as wild beasts, as robbers,
jack-o'-lantern leaping in the shadows of walls,
bells thrilling at the touch of bone fingers,
you come back to abuse and to haunt us,
you, grandfather, and my brother, and the others:
to the forgetful house, yourselves not forgetful,
(for the dead do not forget us, in our hearts
the dead never forget us)
you return to make mischief and to enter the house
you return once more to remind us.
The pumpkin-head lit with a candle, the cry
help the poor, help the poor, help the poor!
comminatory cry from door to door
and the obolos paid that the ghost be laid:
it is our ancestors and children who conspire against us
life unlived and unloved that conspires against us
our neglected hearts and hearths that conspire against us

for we have neglected not only our death
in forgetting our obligations to the dead
we have neglected our living and our children's living
in neglecting our love
for the dead who would still live within us.

III

All summer it rained: day after day, from morning
to sodden noon and eave's-drop eve, it rained:
day after day the heavens and the clouds complained.
Heavy the honeysuckle poll with over-ripe blossom:
rank the myrtle by the doorstep: bleeding the bosom
of the rainsick rose who broke her heart on the tomb.
The dry wells filled, and the vaults, and the cisterns:
and the cellars with underground music: the furrows of clay
glittered with water: rotten under water the wheatfield lay.
In the drear suburb, beyond the greenhouse, and the stonemason's,
on the Cove Road, among the marble shafts and porphyry basins,
and the cold eyeless angels with folded wings,
(there where we fished as children
looking over our shoulders at tombstones)
at last, undermined by water, the headstone fell,
sank softly, slowly, on the grave-mound,
and lay thus, a month neglected, on hollow ground.
And the spirit, the unappeased houseless spirit,
whose dwelling should be in ourselves, those who inherit,
even as our dwelling is in the tomb,
homeward once more looks now for prayer and praise
to be with laurels blest
and in our breast
live out his due bequest of nights and days.

IV

And so it is you at the dark's edge, grandfather,
revenant again to complain and to haunt me,
cavorting at the fire's edge, leaping through the flames,
while the moon, behind Sheepfold Hill,
lights her old bonfire, old bone-fire, and our ancestors
gather down from the hillside, gather up from the sea-wall,

and come home to be warmed. You, from the Geissberg,
the 'Rhine full of molten gold, and the Neckar Valley
echoing the slow psalm of the curfew,'
from 'a lecture by Humboldt,' and a ship at sea
'which, as she took up the winds,
and rose in triumph over the waves,'
was a symbol to you of our relation to god:
'the absolute, the eternal, the infinite, a shoreless sea,
in unconscious rest, all its powers in repose,
to be used at man's will.' And the *Iphigenie*
von Tauris, at Heidelberg read with delight,
while the little Humboldt, 'his small face flushed,
eyes small, bright, and piercing,'
transcribed the last page of his *Kosmos.*
'And I thought, as he moved off, helped by his servant,
had I waited a twelvemonth, I would never have seen him.'

All Hallows' Even, Hallowe'en,
the evening of the last of October,
and the harvest in-gathered:
and the first of November, *Allerheiligen,*
and the second of November, *Allerseelen.*
Was your vision of god not enough, that you come
for the vision of the living, and the cricket's
small share of the hearthstone? Or is it some other,
some humbler, more human, news that you crave?
Your children?—Long dead; and Cousin Abiel, the Quaker;
and the house with the hawthorns torn down;
and your own house a chapel; and the whaleships
departed: no more shines the eagle
on the pilot-house roof at the foot of the hill.

Yet no, not these are your loves, but the timeless and formless,
the laws and the vision: as you saw on the ship
how, like an angel, she subdued to her purpose
the confused power of ocean, the diffused power of wind,
translating them swiftly to beauty,
'so infinite ends, and finite begins, so man
may make the god finite and viable,
make conscious god's powers in action and being.'
Was it so? is it so? and the life so lived?

O you who made magic
under an oak-tree once in the sunlight
translating your acorns to green cups and saucers
for the grandchild mute at the tree's foot,
and died, alone, on a doorstep at midnight
your vision complete but your work undone,
with your dream of a world religion,
'a peace convention of religions, a worship
purified of myth and of dogma:'
dear scarecrow, dear pumpkin-head!
who masquerade now as my child, to assure
the continuing love, the continuing dream,
and the heart and the hearth and the wholeness—
it was so, it is so, and the life so lived
shines this night like the moon over Sheepfold Hill,
and he who interpreted the wonders of god
is himself dissolved and interpreted.
Rest: be at peace. It suffices to know and to rest.
For the singers, in rest, shall stand as a river
whose source is unending forever.

A Letter from Li Po

I

Fanfare of northwest wind, a bluejay wind
announces autumn, and the Equinox
rolls back blue bays to a far afternoon.
Somewhere beyond the Gorge Li Po is gone,
looking for friendship or an old love's sleeve
or writing letters to his children, lost,
and to his children's children, and to us.
What was his light? of lamp or moon or sun?
Say that it changed, for better or for worse,
sifted by leaves, sifted by snow; on mulberry silk
a slant of witch-light; on the pure text
a slant of genius; emptying mind and heart

for winecups and more winecups and more words.
What was his time? Say that it was a change,
but constant as a changing thing may be,
from chicory's moon-dark blue down the taut scale
to chicory's tenderest pink, in a pink field
such as imagination dreams of thought.
But of the heart beneath the winecup moon
the tears that fell beneath the winecup moon
for children lost, lost lovers, and lost friends,
what can we say but that it never ends?
Even for us it never ends, only begins.
Yet to spell down the poem on her page,
margining her phrases, parsing forth
the sevenfold prism of meaning, up the scale
from chicory pink to blue, is to assume
Li Po himself: as he before assumed
the poets and the sages who were his.
Like him, we too have eaten of the word:
with him, are somewhere lost beyond the Gorge:
and write, in rain, a letter to lost children,
a letter long as time and brief as love.

II

And yet not love, not only love. Not caritas
or only that. Nor the pink chicory love,
deep as it may be, even to moon-dark blue,
in which the dragon of his meaning flew
for friends or children lost, or even
for the beloved horse, for Li Po's horse:
not these, in the self's circle so embraced:
too near, too dear, for pure assessment: no,
a letter crammed and creviced, crannied full,
storied and stored as the ripe honeycomb
with other faith than this.
                              As of sole pride
and holy loneliness, the intrinsic face
worn by the always changing shape between
end and beginning, birth and death.
How moves that line of daring on the map?
Where was it yesterday, or where this morning

when thunder struck at seven, and in the bay
the meteor made its dive, and shed its wings,
and with them one more Icarus? Where struck
that lightning-stroke which in your sleep you saw
wrinkling across the eyelid? Somewhere else?
But somewhere else is always here and now.
Each moment crawls that lightning on your eyelid:
each moment you must die. It was a tree
that this time died for you: it was a rock
and with it all its local web of love:
a chimney, spilling down historic bricks:
perhaps a skyful of Ben Franklin's kites.
And with them, us. For we must hear and bear
the news from everywhere: the hourly news,
infinitesimal or vast, from everywhere.

III

Sole pride and loneliness: it is the state
the kingdom rather of all things: we hear
news of the heart in weather of the Bear,
slide down the rungs of Cassiopeia's Chair,
still on the nursery floor, the Milky Way;
and, if we question one, must question all.
What is this 'man'? How far from him is 'me'?
Who, in this conch-shell, locked the sound of sea?
We are the tree, yet sit beneath the tree,
among the leaves we are the hidden bird,
we are the singer and are what is heard.
What is this 'world'? Not Li Po's Gorge alone,
and yet, this too might be. 'The wind was high
north of the White King City, by the fields
of whistling barley under cuckoo sky,'
where, as the silkworm drew her silk, Li Po
spun out his thoughts of us. 'Endless as silk'
(he said) 'these poems for lost loves, and us,'
and, 'for the peachtree, blooming in the ditch.'
Here is the divine loneliness in which
we greet, only to doubt, a voice, a word,
the smoke of sweetfern after frost, a face
touched, and loved, but still unknown, and then

a body, still mysterious in embrace.
Taste lost as touch is lost, only to leave
dust on the doorsill or an ink-stained sleeve:
and yet, for the inadmissible, to grieve.
Of leaf and love, at last, only to doubt:
from world within or world without, kept out.

IV

Caucus of robins on an alien shore
as of the Ho-Ho birds at Jewel Gate
southward bound and who knows where and never late
or lost in a roar at sea. Rovers of chaos
each one the 'Rover of Chao,' whose slight bones
shall put to shame the swords. We fly with these,
have always flown, and they
stay with us here, stand still and stay,
while, exiled in the Land of Pa, Li Po
still at the Wine Spring stoops to drink the moon.
And northward now, for fall gives way to spring,
from Sandy Hook and Kitty Hawk they wing,
and he remembers, with the pipes and flutes,
drunk with joy, bewildered by the chance
that brought a friend, and friendship, how, in vain,
he strove to speak, 'and in long sentences,' his pain.
Exiled are we. Were exiles born. The 'far away,'
language of desert, language of ocean, language of sky,
as of the unfathomable worlds that lie
between the apple and the eye,
these are the only words we learn to say.
Each morning we devour the unknown. Each day
we find, and take, and spill, or spend, or lose,
a sunflower splendor of which none knows the source.
This cornucopia of air! This very heaven
of simple day! We do not know, can never know,
the alphabet to find us entrance there.
So, in the street, we stand and stare,
to greet a friend, and shake his hand,
yet know him beyond knowledge, like ourselves;
ocean unknowable by unknowable sand.

V

The locust tree spills sequins of pale gold
in spiral nebulae, borne on the Invisible
earthward and deathward, but in change to find
the cycles to new birth, new life. Li Po
allowed his autumn thoughts like these to flow,
and, from the Gorge, sends word of Chouang's dream.
Did Chouang dream he was a butterfly?
Or did the butterfly dream Chouang? If so,
why then all things can change, and change again,
the sea to brook, the brook to sea, and we
from man to butterfly; and back to man.
This 'I,' this moving 'I,' this focal 'I,'
which changes, when it dreams the butterfly,
into the thing it dreams of; liquid eye
in which the thing takes shape, but from within
as well as from without: this liquid 'I':
how many guises, and disguises, this
nimblest of actors takes, how many names
puts on and off, the costumes worn but once,
the player queen, the lover, or the dunce,
hero or poet, father or friend,
suiting the eloquence to the moment's end;
childlike, or bestial; the language of the kiss
sensual or simple; and the gestures, too,
as slight as that with which an empire falls,
or a great love's abjured; these feignings, sleights,
savants, or saints, or fly-by-nights,
the novice in her cell, or wearing tights
on the high wire above a hell of lights:
what's true in these, or false? which is the 'I'
of 'I's'? Is it the master of the cadence, who
transforms all things to a hoop of flame, wherethrough
tigers of meaning leap? And are these true,
the language never old and never new,
such as the world wears on its wedding day,
the something borrowed with something chicory blue?
In every part we play, we play ourselves;
even the secret doubt to which we come

249

beneath the changing shapes of self and thing,
yes, even this, at last, if we should call
and dare to name it, we would find
the only voice that answers is our own.
We are once more defrauded by the mind.

Defrauded? No. It is the alchemy by which we grow.
It is the self becoming word, the word
becoming world. And with each part we play
we add to cosmic *Sum* and cosmic sum.
Who knows but one day we shall find,
hidden in the prism at the rainbow's foot,
the square root of the eccentric absolute,
and the concentric absolute to come.

VI

The thousand eyes, the Argus 'I's' of love,
of these it was, in verse, that Li Po wove
the magic cloak for his last going forth,
into the gorge for his adventure north.
What is not seen or said? The cloak of words
loves all, says all, sends back the word
whether from Green Spring, and the yellow bird
'that sings unceasing on the banks of Kiang,'
or 'from the Green Moss Path, that winds and winds,
nine turns for every hundred steps it winds,
up the Sword Parapet on the road to Shuh.'
'Dead pinetrees hang head-foremost from the cliff.
The cataract roars downward. Boulders fall
splitting the echos from the mountain wall.
No voice, save when the nameless birds complain,
in stunted trees, female echoing male;
or, in the moonlight, the lost cuckoo's cry,
piercing the traveller's heart. Wayfarer from afar,
why are you here? what brings you here? why here?'

VII

Why here. Nor can we say why here. The peachtree bough
scrapes on the wall at midnight, the west wind
sculptures the wall of fog that slides

seaward, over the Gulf Stream.
                              The rat
comes through the wainscot, brings to his larder
the twinned acorn and chestnut burr. Our sleep
lights for a moment into dream, the eyes
turn under eyelids for a scene, a scene,
O and the music, too, of landscape lost.
And yet, not lost. For here savannahs wave
cressets of pampas, and the kingfisher
binds all that gold with blue.
                              Why here? why here?
Why does the dream keep only this, just this—?
Yes, as the poem or the music do?

The timelessness of time takes form in rhyme:
the lotus and the locust tree rehearse
a four-form song, the quatrain of the year:
not in the clock's chime only do we hear
the passing of the Now into the past,
the passing into future of the Now:
but in the alteration of the bough
time becomes visible, becomes audible,
becomes the poem and the music too:
time becomes still, time becomes time, in rhyme.
Thus, in the Court of Aloes, Lady Yang
called the musicians from the Pear Tree Garden,
called for Li Po, in order that the spring,
tree-peony spring, might so be made immortal.
Li Po, brought drunk to court, took up his brush,
but washed his face among the lilies first,
then wrote the song of Lady Flying Swallow:
which Hsuang Sung, the emperor, forthwith played,
moving quick fingers on a flute of jade.
Who will forget that afternoon? Still, still,
the singer holds his phrase, the rising moon
remains unrisen. Even the fountain's falling blade
hangs in the air unbroken, and says: Wait!

VIII

Text into text, text out of text. Pretext
for scholars or for scholiasts. The living word

springs from the dying, as leaves in spring
spring from dead leaves, our birth from death.
And all is text, is holy text. Sheepfold Hill
becomes its name for us, and yet is still
unnamed, unnamable, a book of trees
before it was a book for men or sheep,
before it was a book for words. Words, words,
for it is scarlet now, and brown, and red,
and yellow where the birches have not shed,
where, in another week, the rocks will show.
And in this marriage of text and thing how can we know
where most the meaning lies? We climb the hill
through bullbriar thicket and the wild rose, climb
past poverty-grass and the sweet-scented bay
scaring the pheasant from his wall, but can we say
that it is only these, through these, we climb,
or through the words, the cadence, and the rhyme?
Chang Hsu, calligrapher of great renown,
needed to put but his three cupfuls down
to tip his brush with lightning. On the scroll,
wreaths of cloud rolled left and right, the sky
opened upon Forever. Which is which?
The poem? Or the peachtree in the ditch?
Or is all one? Yes, all is text, the immortal text,
Sheepfold Hill the poem, the poem Sheepfold Hill,
and we, Li Po, the man who sings, sings as he climbs,
transposing rhymes to rocks and rocks to rhymes.
The man who sings. What is this man who sings?
And finds this dedicated use for breath
for phrase and periphrase of praise between
the twin indignities of birth and death?
Li Yung, the master of the epitaph,
forgetting about meaning, who himself
had added 'meaning' to the book of 'things,'
lies who knows where, himself sans epitaph,
his text, too, lost, forever lost . . .
                                    And yet, no,
text lost and poet lost, these only flow
into that other text that knows no year.
The peachtree in the poem is still here.
The song is in the peachtree and the car.

I

The winds of doctrine blow both ways at once.
The wetted finger feels the wind each way,
presaging plums from north, and snow from south.
The dust-wind whistles from the eastern sea
to dry the nectarine and parch the mouth.
The west wind from the desert wreathes the rain
too late to fill our wells, but soon enough,
the four-day rain that bears the leaves away.
Song with the wind will change, but is still song
and pierces to the rightness in the wrong
or makes the wrong a rightness, a delight.
Where are the eager guests that yesterday
thronged at the gate? Like leaves, they could not stay,
the winds of doctrine blew their minds away,
and we shall have no loving-cup tonight.
No loving-cup: for not ourselves are here
to entertain us in that outer year,
where, so they say, we see the Greater Earth.
The winds of doctrine blow our minds away,
and we are absent till another birth.

X

Beyond the Sugar Loaf, in the far wood,
under the four-day rain, gunshot is heard
and with the falling leaf the falling bird
flutters her crimson at the huntsman's foot.
Life looks down at death, death looks up at life,
the eyes exchange the secret under rain,
rain all the way from heaven: and all three
know and are known, share and are shared, a silent
moment of union and communion.
                            Have we come
this way before, and at some other time?
Is it the Wind Wheel Circle we have come?
We know the eye of death, and in it too
the eye of god, that closes as in sleep,
giving its light, giving its life, away:

clouding itself as consciousness from pain,
clouding itself, and then, the shutter shut.
And will this eye of god awake again?
Or is this what he loses, loses once,
but always loses, and forever lost?
It is the always and unredeemable cost
of his invention, his fatigue. The eye
closes, and no other takes its place.
It is the end of god, each time, each time.
Yet, though the leaves must fall, the galaxies
rattle, detach, and fall, each to his own
perplexed and individual death, Lady Yang
gone with the inkberry's vermilion stalk,
the peony face behind a fan of frost,
the blue-moon eyebrow behind a fan of rain,
beyond recall by any alchemist
or incantation from the Book of Change:
unresumable, as, on Sheepfold Hill,
the fir cone of a thousand years ago:
still, in the loving, and the saying so,
as when we name the hill, and, with the name,
bestow an essence, and a meaning, too:
do we endow them with our lives?
                              They move
into another orbit: into a time
not theirs: and we become the bell to speak
this time: as we become new eyes
with which they see, the voice
in which they find duration, short or long,
the chthonic and hermetic song.
                              Beyond Sheepfold Hill,
gunshot again, the bird flies forth to meet
predestined death, to look with conscious sight
into the eye of light
the light unflinching that understands and loves.
And Sheepfold Hill accepts them, and is still.

                    XI

The landscape and the language are the same.
And we ourselves are language and are land,

together grew with Sheepfold Hill, rock, and hand,
and mind, all taking substance in a thought
wrought out of mystery: birdflight and air
predestined from the first to be a pair:
as, in the atom, the living rhyme
invented her divisions, which in time,
and in the terms of time, would make and break
the text, the texture, and then all remake.
This powerful mind that can by thinking take
the order of the world and all remake,
will it, for joy in breaking, break instead
its own deep thought that thought itself be dead?
Already in our coil of rock and hand,
hidden in the cloud of mind, burning, fading,
under the waters, in the eyes of sand,
was that which in its time would understand.
Already in the Kingdom of the Dead
the scrolls were waiting for the names and dates
and what would there irrevocably be said.
The brush was in the hand, the poem was in the love,
the praise was in the word. The 'Book of Lives'
listed the name, Li Po, as an Immortal;
and it was time to travel. Not, this year,
north to the Damask City, or the Gorge,
but, by the phoenix borne, swift as the wind,
to the Jade Palace Portal. There
look through the clouded to the clear
and there watch evil like a brush-stroke disappear
in the last perfect rhyme
of the begin-all-end-all poem, time.

XII

Northwest by north. The grasshopper weathervane
bares to the moon his golden breastplate, swings
in his predicted circle, gilded legs and wings
bright with frost, predicting frost. The tide
scales with moon-silver, floods the marsh, fulfils
Payne Creek and Quivett Creek, rises to lift
the fishing-boats against a jetty wall;
and past them floods the plankton and the weed

255

and limp sea-lettuce for the horseshoe crab
who sleeps till daybreak in his nest of reed.
The hour is open as the mind is open.
Closed as the mind is closed. Opens as the hand opens
to receive the ghostly snowflakes of the moon, closes
to feel the sunbeams of the bloodstream warm
our human inheritance of touch. The air tonight
brings back, to the all-remembering world, its ghosts,
borne from the Great Year on the Wind Wheel Circle.
On that invisible wave we lift, we too,
and drag at secret moorings,
stirred by the ancient currents that gave us birth.

And they are here, Li Po and all the others,
our fathers and our mothers: the dead leaf's footstep
touches the grass: those who were lost at sea
and those the innocents the too-soon dead:

                    all mankind
and all it ever knew is here in-gathered,
held in our hands, and in the wind
breathed by the pines on Sheepfold Hill.

                    How still
the Quaker Graveyard, the Meeting House how still,
where Cousin Abiel, on a night like this,
now long since dead, but then how young, how young,
scuffing among the dead leaves after frost
looked up and saw the Wine Star, listened and heard
borne from all quarters the Wind Wheel Circle word:
the father within him, the mother within him, the self
coming to self through love of each for each.
In this small mute democracy of stones
is it Abiel or Li Po who lies
and lends us against death our speech?
They are the same, and it is both who teach.
The poets and the prophecies are ours:
and these are with us as we turn, in turn,
the leaves of love that fill the Book of Change.

Another Lycidas

I

Yet once more in the empty room review
the photomatic photo on the table
which years have faded but from which
still behind owlish glasses stubborn eyes
under an ancient hatbrim fix your own.
                         Which nevertheless are his
since it is at a camera that he gazes
there in the railway station, his own image
rounded in a lens in a curtained cubicle
while outside, along an echoing concourse,
passengers hurry for trains and trains depart
                         and overhead
the silent clock the electric clock
                         sans tick *sans* tock
with quivering hand pricks off another second
advancing for his life a last October.
                         Yet once more view
the silent face whose fierce regard for you
follows you like a conscience: stubborn, sober,
who after two martinis waits
and thus kills time till the opening of the gates.
What train it is he waits for we well know.
Leaving behind the evening suburbs it will go
south to the Islands and the pinewood Cape
where he was born, and grew, and knew
as if it were a legend learned by heart
each name each house each village, that ancient land
familiar to him as his face, the land
whence came with the ancestral name
inheritance of those steadfast eyes, the hand
salt-stung salt-harsh that for his forebears threw
the barbed harpoon or turned the wheel to windward
and kept it by the compass true.

II

Bequeathing us this gimcrack photo
as he himself would say *pictore ignoto*
for contemplation now that he is dead
bequeathing it by accident and not intent
yet speaking to us still and of that day:
what else would he have said or what else say?
                    The massive head
and proud mustachios are not in his regard
and it is not at these he stares
who midway in his life no longer cares
(nel mezzo del cammin di nostra vita)
for vanity of self: what there he sees
and with his vision frees
beyond the Islands and the ancestral seas
and the hall bedroom the humble furnished room
in which he lived until he died:
                  beyond all these
is what he sees he has himself become
and, with him, us: and further still
what, out of yeoman courage, country skill,
the ploughshare patience, the seafarer's will,
has come, as for the sailor homeward bound,
a change of course.
                Profound:
and yet not so, since simple must to complex grow.
And he who as a boy trapped muskrats in the creek
or through snow-stippled poverty-grass
tramped to the ringing pond to fish through ice
or rolled the barrel in, to salt the pork,
or sawed and split the pine and oak
in the pale sweetgrass by the cedar swamp
under a harvest moon that rose again
to silhouette the weathervane
above the meetinghouse: and who would say
year after year when he returned
the 'frost is on the punkin',' or 'I know
clam chowders on the backs of kitchen stoves

that have been there for nigh a hundred years':
                         or in the slate-cold churchyard,
where now unmarked he lies, point out the stone
on which appear these words alone:
'The Chinese woman, name unknown': then tell
her story, and a hundred others, which each house
bespoke for him along a mile of elm-tree-shaded road:
                         he who from this had grown
and all this wood-lot lore had known
and never had forgotten, nevertheless
with this rich knowledge also took
to Buenos Aires Cadiz and the rest
                         and Harvard too
his boyhood's book, the scholar's book,
the book that was his life. This was to be
his change of course. What his forefathers learned
of wisdom, courage, skill, on land or sea,
rounding the whalespout horn, or in a summer's 'tempest,'
or 'burning off' in spring or sanding down a bog
or making the strict entries in a log
beneath the swinging lamp, in a clear script
the latitude and longitude: this now would change
and the sea-change reverse. Chapter and verse
replace the log, and ripened scholarship
the island packet and the blue-water ship.

III

Humility was in that furnished room
as in the furnished room that was his mind.
The glass of sharpened pencils on the table
the pencil-sharpener on the windowsill
a row of well-worn books upon a bench
some Spanish and some French
the page-proofs spread out to be worked upon
a few whodunits and a lexicon
                         in a top drawer
a flask of bourbon or the full-ripened corn
for those who *might* be to the manner born
                         behind a curtain
the neatly folded clothes on hangers hung

an old guitar somewhat unstrung
and in its leather case upon the shelf
the top hat now no longer worn
                    tarnished for certain
but much used in more prosperous days.
                    An 'aluminium' kettle
sat in the corner behind his chair, for tea,
                    beside it a red apple.
And the tea-leaves went down the W.C.

                    Evening, by the Esplanade.
Sunset brindles the bridge, the evening star
pierces the cirrus over Chestnut Hill
                    and we are still
asking the twilight question. Where shall it be:
tonight, tonight again, where shall it be?
                    Down 'Mulberry' Street
beckon the streetlights, and our feet
                    through rain or snow or sleet
once more in unison to eastward turn
not to Priapus Garden or to view
what the 'poast' says is 'plaid' today
                    but if burlesque be on
to the Old Howard, or the Tam or Nip
the Oyster House or Silver Dollar Bar
then to the Athens, there once more to meet
with Piston's whole-tone wit or Wheelwright's neat
while the martinis flow and clams are sweet
and he himself our morning star
until Apollo's taxi ploughs the dawn.

                    Who would not mourn
for such a Lycidas? He did not know
himself to sing or build the lofty rhyme
or so he would himself have said: and yet
this was not true: for in him grew
the poet's vision like a tree of light
                    and leaves of light
were in him as the gift of tongues
                    and he was of those few
who, as he heard, reshaped the Word,

and made the poem or the music true:
and he was generous with what he knew.
                    Lightly, lightly, November,
the third unknown by him, with sunshot gale
from the Great Cove or Follins Pond bring home
the hawk and heron: while we remember
                    the untold wealth he took
into the grave with him, the open book
that lies beneath the grass
of all he knew and was:
                    composed by him
with calligraphic hand and curious eye
the pencil point unhurried, fine,
unfolding still its classic line
and waiting still for us to see:
and, at the end, the signet signature, 'G.B.'

Death's but a progress, or so Whitehead says.
The infant dies to childhood the child to boy
the boy to youth the youth to man.
                    Try as we can
if we should think to try or makeshift make
                    we cannot take
one age into another. Life is a span
which like the bridge the link not knowing link
comes to an end in earth as it began.
                    We cannot think
end and beginning all at once but only
in the broken beam of light recall
the instant prism in a recession of successions.
And it is only we, the living, who can see
in such another instant of successions
                    the span of such a man.

The Crystal

I

What time is it now, brother Pythagoras, by the pale stone
set like a jewel in the brow of Sheepfold Hill?
There where the little spider, your geometrist,
shrinks from autumn in the curl of a leaf,
his torn world blown in the wind? What time, tonight,
under the motionless mill-wheel, in the pouring brook,
which bears to the sea—O *thalassa, thalassa,*
pasa thalassa, for the sea is still the sea—
the flickering fins, unnumbered, which will return thence
in April or May? By the dial in Samos what hour?
Or in Babylon among the Magi?
                              Your forefoot ploughs
over the floating Pole Star, Ionian foam
wets once again the gemmed sandal, as westward still
the oars beat time, and the sail runs out, in the wake
of Samian Kolaios.
                    Not you for bars of silver,
nor to trade wool or wine or raisins for tin,
and not to return to Samos, nor with regret, but rather—
listen!—as with these migrants who now above us
whirl the night air with clamor of wings and voices,
southward voyaging, the caucus of robins,
choosing, like you, a propitious hour.
                              So the page turns
always in the middle of a sentence, the beginning of a meaning;
the poem breaks in two. So the prayer, the invocation,
and the revelation, are suspended in our lives,
suspended in a thought. Just as now,
still there in the dark at the prow of your galley,
your hand on the cleat, you observe the division of water,

the division of phosphor, yourself the divider,
and the law in the wave, and the law in the eye;
observing, too, with delight; and remembering
how once on the headland of Bathy at daybreak
you sacrificed a hundred oxen to your godfather, Apollo,
or was it forty or fifty,
and the occasion for it: your vision
of the triangle's godgiven secret, the song of the square
echoing the squares.
                    Long ago: far away:
wave-length and trough-length: the little Pan's Pipe
plaintive and sweet on the water at midnight:
yet audible still to the infinitesimal
tambourine of the eardrum. And now you are sixty,
the beard is of sea-moss. At Delphi
you set foot on the salt shingle, climbed
up the path through the rocks to the temple,
where priestesses dreamed with their oakleaves.
What warning or promise from the *tripous?* What cryptic
oracle flung from the sun on the mountain
to bear on the sea-track that beats to the west?
Daybreak it was, with long shadows. Far down,
at the foot of the gorge, you could measure
the toy groves of olives, the hearse-plumes of cypress,
and daisies danced in a ring, and the poppies
in the grass and wild thyme around you
went running, and crackling like fire. Alas!
a few columns, only, still stand there,
and the wild fig roots in the wall. And now,
your galleys hush west on the sea,
as you, old migrant, set sail once again
(like those fins down the stairs to the bay)
with your wife and your sons, and the grandchildren swaddled,
your gear and your goats and your handmaids;
setting forth as aforetime to Thebes.
                    While we,
secret and silent, sealed off in the west,
sit still and await you. In a different world,
and yet foreseen in your crystal:
the numbers known to your golden abacus,
and the strings that corded your lyre.

Six o'clock, here, in the western world, a west
unknown to sailor Kolaios, or the porters of Tartessus.
Stony Brook ferries its fins to the sea. Four bells
sing now in the fisherman's lighted cabin
above the brass binnacle and the floating compass.
Six o'clock in the cone of the Equinox, the bells
echo over mud-flats, sift through the nets
where mackerel flap and flash in the pools,
and over the oyster-beds, the shells of the razor-fish,
borne inland, to be echoed again
by the austere bell in the puritan steeple.
At seven, in the ancient farmhouse,
cocktails sparkle on the tray, the careful answer
succeeds the casual question, a reasoned dishevelment
ruffling quietly the day's or the hour's issue.
Our names, those we were born with,
or those we were not born with, since all are born nameless,
become the material, or the figment, if we wish,
of which to weave, and then unweave, ourselves.
Our lives, those we inherited, of which
none can claim ownership in fee simple, but only
a tenant's lease, of unpredictable duration,
rented houses from which have already departed perhaps
those others, our other selves, the children:
ourselves in these on our way beyond death
to become the undying succession of inheritors:
these and other aspects of the immortal moment
glow into consciousness for laughter or tears,
an instant of sympathy or misunderstanding, an exchange
of human touch or tact, or agreement, soon silent.
And here, as in the silence, too, that follows,
like the peacock's eye of shadow round the lifted candle,
is the tacit acceptance of death. We invoke,
and what is life but an invocation,
the shore beyond the vortex, the light beyond the dark,
the number beneath the name. We shall not be here
to pour the bright cocktails, while we listen
to the throb of migrant wings in the night air,

the chorus of departing voices, the bells from the bay;
and yet, brother Pythagoras, like you,
who still set your sail this night to the west,
we too shall be held so. After our deaths
we too shall be held so. And thus, brought together.

III

And yet, if this were so, but in another sense:
the immortality, perhaps, of a different sort:
or death somehow of a different kind: and if it were true,
as in the myth of All Hallows at this season,
when frost beards the pumpkin, and the last apple
thuds to bare earth; and if, from our graves,
whether at Metapontum by the fields of corn,
or by the muddy river at Isle of Hope,
or under the Acropolis on the hill of rocks,
with the moon's shield brazen above us: yes, if, called by name,
you there, I here, we could arise,
and make our way in the dark to the road's edge
for a day or a night of the familiar habits;
what time would it be, brother Pythagoras,
for what custom, and what place?
                              All life
is ritual, or becomes so: the elusive pattern
unfolds its arcanum of observances,
measured in time, and measured by time, as the heartbeat
measures the blood. Each action, no matter how simple,
is precious in itself, as part of the devotion,
our devotion to life. And what part of this ritual
would we choose for reenactment? What rite
single out to return for? After the long silence,
and the long sleep, wherein has been never
configuration of dream; no light, no shape;
not the geometer's triangle, flashing in sun,
to be resolved in reason, no, nor the poet's mirage of landscape,
brilliant as the image in the finder of a camera,
nor the gem-carver's little emerald, with lyre and cupido,
or the sculptor's bronze, the *cire-perdue*,
an art fetched from Egypt: no, no sound, no color:

what then would we choose? Carver of gems, lover of crystal,
savior-god of Croton! can you yet soothsay?

Easy enough, it would be, to find in the darkness
the familiar roadside, the shape of a known tree,
and then, how naturally, alas, the faded signpost
stuck in the sand: and on it to make out with joy
the names that point homeward. And easy enough
to fly then as the bee flies, to home as to hive.
And arrived there, to find the door open,
the fire on the hearth, the pot on the trivet,
the dish on the table—with a red rim—for grapes,
and the ripe blue cluster; to feel with one's foot
the slope of the floorboard, and on it the scars
ridged by the adze; the shelves bright with bowls,
and the floor bright with mats, and the walls
bright with pictures. And then, to lift gently
the one thing most loved: as if in this thing
one could best hold them all. And thus, it might be
a spoon from one's childhood: a shell of thin silver,
a handle shaped like a tiny brick chimney,
atop of it, perching, a dwarf with a horn,
a curled horn tilted to heaven.
                      In this,
to achieve the resumption, the chained implication,
backward, then forward, of the whole of one's life.

Too simple perhaps? Or an example, only.
For, to which house, of the many houses,
and all of them loved, would one fare first?
To which altar of the many altars, the changing
gods, with their changing attributes? Which city
of the many dear cities? Samos, with its wall,
and the port, and the Hera Temple, and the tunnel
carved through the rock by Eupalinos, to bring water
for the three brave fountains, praised by Herodotus?
Or Croton, of the Brotherhood? Who can say?
Perhaps for none of these, but, more simply,
for the pronunciation, softly, of a single name:
the observation, precisely, of a single flower:
white crocus, white hyacinth. Or perhaps
we would return if only once more to remember

something secret and precious, but forgotten: something intended,
but never performed: begun, but not finished.
Or else, to notice, but now with a more careful love,
the little hooked claws, bent down, of the clover:
the white geometry, in clearest numbers,
of those little asters, or asterisks, the snow.
Samples, examples!
And perhaps too concrete. The heart might so choose,
but what of the mind? All very well
the sight or the sound, the taste or the feeling, the touch
or the texture. And, as in a dream,
To combine them—delicious! Thus, a ring of your father's,
Mnesarchos, the gem-carver: you watch him at work,
yourself still a boy, and both silent:
the emerald held in a vice, then the green
ice of the clear stone gives up its goddess,
the tiny wave bears up its Venus, green foam
on the brow and the shoulder. The image?
Of course! But beneath or behind it
the knowledge, the craft: and the art, above all.
Would it not be for this, for ruler and compass,
brother Pythagoras, that we would return?

For both: the one is the other. In each lies the other.
Design shines implicit in the blind moment
of self-forgetful perception: belief is steadfast
in the putting forth of a hand, as in the first
wingbeat, or extension of a claw; the law
unfolding and infolding forever.
It would be for this
Apollonian fountain of the forever unfolding,
the forever-together, ourselves but a leaf
on the fountain of tree, that we would return:
the crystal self-shaping, the godhead designing the god.
For this moment of vision, we would return.

IV

The admirations come early, crowd through
the lenses of light and the lenses of the eye,
such sudden and inimitable shapes, such colors
confusing and confused, the vast but orderly

267

outpouring and downpouring and inpouring—who but
a god could distribute so many and so various,
but what god and where? Not Aladdin
in the dark cave walking on jewels and precious stones,
on diamonds and rubies, brushing the walls
of topaz and opal, ever went among such wonders
or was ever so dazzled. The wind's serpent
sibilant and silver in a field of barley
insinuates a pattern, the concentric
ripples in a fountain perpetuate another
the quartz crystal offers a pyramid, and two together,
joined, a cube! Where burns not or shines not
purity of line? The veins of the myrtle
are alive with it, the carpenter's board
diagrams it in a cross-section of history, life
empanelled golden in a design. What does not your hand
turn up or over, living or inanimate,
large or small, that does not signal
the miracle of interconnectedness
the beams meeting and crossing in the eye and the mind
as also in the sun? How can you set end to it
where is no ending and no beginning
save in the one that becomes the many, the many
that compose the one? How shall we praise the forms?
Algebra shines, the rose-tree perfects with precision
its love the rose, the rose perfects with precision
its love the seed, the seed perfects with precision
its love the tree. How shall we praise the numbers?
Geometry measures an arc of orchard an arc of sky
the inward march and arch of the mind. Things
are numbers. Numbers are the shape
given to things, immanent in things past and present
as in the things to come. Not water nor fire
nor Anaximander's cloud nor only
the inexhaustible and unknowable flux which Heraclitus
in vain exhorted to be still, but number
that buds and breaks from number, unfolds in number,
blossoms in number, is born and dies in number.

And the sounds too, your loves the sounds:
In these to find the final of harmonies, the seven

unequal strings of the lyre, the seven notes to be
intertwined or countered, doubled or trebled or wreathed;
seven strings for the seven sages, to each
the *tripous* awarded, as to Pherekydes your teacher:
but not to yourself, except in
the little tripod of silver you minted
for the coins of Croton. And then, ringing all,
encircling the worlds and the god's central fire,
the revolving spheres and the music they chorus
too perfect for hearing.
                              The admirations
come early, stay long, multiply marvelously,
as if of their own volition. In such confusion
what answer for order? The odd and the even,
the prime and the solid, the plane and the oblong:
numbers, shapes, sounds, measurements, all these
to be studied and observed with joy, with passion,
the wind's serpent to be followed where it
vanishes in a spiral of silver through the wheatfield
the ripples to be pursued as they ply outward
over the fountain-face of cloud-flattering water
plangency and pitch of the lyre's note
to be judged exactly by the length of the tight string
notched in the edge of the tortoise-shell:
crystal and asphodel and snowflake
alike melting in the palm of the mind, and the mind
admiring its own admirations, in these too
uncovering the miracle of number: all, at last,
transparent, inward and outward, the one
everlasting of experience, a pure delight.

                    v

What is the voyage and who is the voyager?
Who is it now hoisting the sail
casting off the rope and running out the oars
the helmsman with his hand on the tiller
and his eyes turned to windward? What time is it now
in the westward pour of the worlds and the westward
pour of the mind? Like a centipede on a mirror
the galley stands still in a blaze of light

and yet swims forward: on the mirror of eternity
glitters like a golden scarab: and the ranked oars
strike down in harmony beat down in unison
churn up the water to phosphor and foam
and yet like the galley are still.
                                          So you
still stand there, your hand on the tiller,
at the center of your thought, which is timeless,
yourself become crystal. While we,
still locked in the west, yet are present before you,
and wait and are silent.
                                    In the ancient farmhouse
which has now become your temple
we listen again to the caucus of robins
the whistle of migrant voices and wings
the turn of the great glass of season.
You taught the migration of souls: all things
must continue, since numbers are deathless:
the mind, like these migrants, crosses all seasons,
and thought, like these cries, is immortal.
The cocktails sparkle, are an oblation.
We pour for the gods, and will always,
you there, we here, and the others who follow,
pour thus in communion. Separate in time,
and yet not separate. Making oblation
in a single moment of consciousness
to the endless forever-together.
                                          This night
we all set sail for the west.

Index of First Lines

High on the southern wall the clock   90
How shall we praise the magnificence of the dead   36
I am a house, says Senlin, locked and darkened   20
I read the primrose and the sea   142
I saw all these things and they meant nothing   174
If man, that angel of bright consciousness   156
In secret wood, where once he stood   227
In the clear shaft of light the child so standing   163
Insist on formality if you will, let the skeleton   171
It is a shabby backdrop of bright stars   79
It is the other, it is the separate, it is the one   184
It was of a deck, the prow of a ship, uplifted   185
it's a fine boy, not a blemish, God bless him   85
Listen: the ancient voices hail us from the farther shore   236
Music will more nimbly move   179
Mysticism, but let us have no words   159
No, I shall not say why it is that I love you   10
Northward, the nothing that we give a name   84
Not with despair, nor with rash hardihood   132
Not with the noting of a private hate   166
Nothing to say, you say? Then we'll say nothing   140
Observe yourself, but placidly: the mirror   180
On that wild verge in the late light he stood   162
One cricket said to another—   151
One skeleton-leaf, white-ribbed, a last year's leaf   56
Or daylong watched, in the kaleidoscope   131
Out of your sickness let your sickness speak—   148
Pawn to king four; pawn to king four; pawn   136
Rimbaud and Verlaine, precious pair of poets   141
Sad softness of control, unceasing censor   154
Said Railway Willy, O carry me back   233
sallow and somewhat haggard; thin and pallid   99
Senlin sat before us and we heard him   34
Senlin sits before us, and we see him   12
Sleep: and between the closed eyelids of sleep   116
smoke Sweet Caporals   87
So, in the evening, to the simple cloister   124
So this is you   93
Stood, at the closed door, and remembered—   139
Surround the thing with phrases, and perceptions   166
Take then the music; plunge in the thickest of it,—   45
tell the tale silverly   109

272